GUIDE TO THE RECORDS OF NORWICH CATHEDRAL

This is a summary guide only and does not include material deposited at the NRO after 1998.

For a full catalogue, including more recently deposited material, see the on-line catalogue NROCAT at http://www.archives.norfolk.gov.uk/nroindex.htm

by

Frank Meeres, B.D., D.A.A.,
Dean and Chapter Archivist
Norfolk Record Office

Norfolk Record Office
1998

First published 1998 by Norfolk Record Office. Obtainable from Norfolk Record Office, Gildengate House, Anglia Square, Upper Green Lane, Norwich, NR3 1AX.

J.R. Alban, B.A., Ph.D., D.A.A., *County Archivist.*

ISBN 0 903103 09 5

Printed by Rigby Print, Norwich.

CONTENTS

THE CATHEDRAL

The records described here are those of the priory of the Holy Trinity, Norwich, and its successor body the Dean and Chapter of Norwich Cathedral. They were deposited by the Dean and Chapter in the Norfolk Record Office on 29 January 1975. The episcopal records of Norwich diocese, also held by the Norfolk Record Office, are a separate archive and are not described here.

The Benedictine priory of the Holy Trinity was founded by Bishop Herbert Losinga on his removal of the seat of the bishopric from Thetford. According to the chronicler, Matthew Paris (followed by the Norwich chronicler Bartholomew Cotton), this took place on 9 April 1094, but it was moreprobably at some time in 1095 (see B. Dodwell, 'The Foundation of Norwich Cathedral', *Transactions of the Royal Historical Society*, 5th ser., vii (1957), 1-18). The priory had a population of about 60 monks and, by the mid twelfth century, had small dependent cells at St Leonards in Thorpe, Yarmouth, Lynn, and Aldeby in Norfolk and at Hoxne in Suffolk. It also administered the hospital of St Paul in Norwich. Bishop Herbert granted estates to the priory, including the profits of the Whitsun fair at Norwich, the manors of Hindolveston, Hindringham, Hemsby and Martham, and parts of the manor of Thorpe next Norwich. King Henry I had granted the latter to the bishop for the expenses of building the new cathedral, but Herbert retained part of it, giving to the monks instead the manor of Gnatingdon in Sedgeford and land in Thornham and Mintlyn. The largest early grants by private persons were the manor of Trowse Newton, given by Godric, and the manor of Eaton, given by Alan son of Flaald. By the fourteenth century, the priory had sixteen large estates - Plumstead, Monks' Grange (in Pockthorpe on the edge of Norwich), Eaton, Catton, Hindolveston, Hindringham, North Elmham, Gateley, Thornham, Trowse Newton, Hemsby, Martham, Taverham, Gnatingdon and Sedgeford, all in Norfolk, and Denham in Suffolk: these were known as the prior's manors. It had smaller estates and rights in churches in about thirty parishes in the city of Norwich and about 100 parishes in Norfolk and Suffolk, as well as at Chalk in Kent and Scampton in Lincolnshire.

The monastery was dissolved by Henry VIII and a capitular body of dean and prebendaries or canons established: the estates of the former priory were granted to them. There was considerable continuity of personnel: the last prior became the first dean, five of the six prebendaries were former monks and sixteen more of the monks became minor canons or lay clerks. However, the surrender to Henry VIII was considered to be invalid because the bishop of Norwich (as successor to the founder) had not given his consent. The chapter surrendered to Edward VI, who reformed the capitular body granting to it most but not all of the estates they previously held: some, such as the manor of Hemsby, were kept by the Crown and later sold, but the Cathedral also gained some estates, such as the rectory of Scalby in Yorkshire, formerly belonging to Bridlington priory. The cathedral was originally governed by statutes of Henry VIII. In 1619, Bishop Harsnett stated that no statutes had been legalised by Edward VI, Mary or Elizabeth I: King James I therefore formally issued a body of statutes on 9 August 1620 and the Cathedral was from then governed by these.

The Dean and Chapter was abolished by Parliament in 1649 and by Act of Parliament cathedral estates were seized for sale on 30 April 1649. Cathedral records were then stored centrally with episcopal records in London. In November 1660, Parliament declared all sales of church land during the Commonwealth period void. Records of dioceses and cathedrals were transferred to Lambeth Palace and there sorted before being returned to their respective reinstated owners. Inevitably, there was some intermixing of the archives and over the last hundred years medieval records have been returned to Norwich from Canterbury, Lincoln, Hereford and Windsor.

The priory had peculiar rights (exempt from the jurisdiction of the archdeacon, but not that of the bishop) over the parishes of Arminghall, West Beckham, Catton, Eaton, Hindolveston, Martham, Lakenham, Great Plumstead, Sedgeford, Sprowston, Trowse Newton, Hemsby, Hindringham, Scratby, Taverham, Winterton, all in Norfolk, and the parishes of St Helen, St Mary in the Marsh, St James Pockthorpe and St Paul in Norwich. After the Reformation, the dean and chapter had peculiar jurisdiction over these parishes, apart from Hemsby, Hindringham, Scratby, Taverham and Winterton. Many of the records of this peculiar jurisdiction passed to diocesan officials and are listed among the diocesan and probate archives, but some material remained with the cathedral archives and is described in this guide.

The priory had jurisdiction over the cathedral precinct and before 1524 claimed it over other parts of Norwich, although this was disputed by the city. Jurisdiction over the leet of Newgate (Surrey Street) was granted to the citizens in 1305. The priory continued to claim jurisdiction over Tombland, Raton Row, and Holme Street (all just outside the cathedral precinct), St Paul's parish and Magdalen Hospital, while it also claimed the right to hold a fair on Tombland each Whitsun and rights over grazing land at Eaton and Lakenham. By agreement made under award of Cardinal Wolsey in 1524, the priory gave 80 acres of land (later called Town Close) in Eaton to the city and the city surrendered its claim to grazing rights elsewhere in Eaton and Lakenham. The priory also surrendered its right to hold the fair and its claim to jurisdiction beyond the precinct. After the Reformation, the dean and chapter held sessions courts with jurisdiction over the precinct, including that of coroner.

The history of the Cathedral is described in *Norwich Cathedral: City, Church and Diocese, 1096-1996,* ed. I. Atherton and others (London, 1996). The architectural history is given in detail in E. C. Fernie, *An Architectural History of Norwich Cathedral* (Oxford, 1993).

THE RECORDS

The main series of pre-Reformation records are: deeds of title - royal, papal, archiepiscopal, episcopal and private grants or confirmations of grants to estates and to churches [DCN 41-45]; cartularies, known in Norwich as registers, with which are included a fourteenth-century letter book [DCN 40]; obedientiary rolls - account rolls of the monastic officials recording income and expenditure on the estates and churches in their care and the expenses which were the responsibilities of their department [DCN 1]; account rolls for the dependent cells and for the hospital of St Paul in Norwich [DCN 2]; bailiffs' accounts and manor court rolls for the sixteen prior's manors and a smaller quantity for other cathedral estates [DCN 60-66]; rentals, surveys, and extents of the estates [DCN 51, 52]; accounts for charities [DCN 4]; acta and comperta rolls - visitation records of parishes within the jurisdiction of the priory on which wills are endorsed [DCN 67]; records concerning legal disputes with the city and other institutions about jurisdictional rights [DCN 84-89]. Pre-Reformation records among the collection not related to the cathedral include records of the bishopric and of St Benet's Abbey [DCN 40/8, DCN 95]; deeds of other religious houses in East Anglia [DCN 46]; title deeds for episcopal and private estates that have become mixed with the cathedral title deeds [DCN 44]; records of ecclesiastical and lay taxation including the ninth of 1297 [DCN 5-8]; an account roll of the steward of the Great Hospital, Norwich, 1515 [DCN 9/4]; and a deposited account roll of the debtors of Alderman Robert Toppes of Norwich *c.*1467 [DCN 9/5] (an endorsement records that this was placed in the priory in 1492.)

The main series of post-Reformation records are the cathedral statutes [DCN 27]; chapter act books and supporting papers [DCN 24-26]; treasurer's and receiver's accounts, audit books with related financial records and bundles of audit papers [DCN 10-23]; registers of leases of estates, known as ledger books, which also include institutions to benefices in the gift of the cathedral, patents and miscellaneous material [DCN 47]; rentals, surveys and valuations of estates including the Parliamentary Survey of 1649 [DCN 51, 52]; estate leases and papers [DCN 48-59] containing much miscellaneous material including a building account for the house of Sir John Fastolf at Earlham of the fifteenth century [DCN 59/11], the farming account book of a Mr Aldrich of Eaton, 1664-7 [DCN 59/12/13], Wacton vestry minutes and poor rate accounts, 1769-1798 [DCN 59/40], water colours of Fring parsonage [DCN 49/19/6]; maps and plans [DCN 127]; records of appointments of cathedral officials [DCN 30-39]; patent books recording diocesan appointments and leases which were subject to confirmation by the dean and chapter [DCN 93]; documents concerning the cathedral fabric from the seventeenth to the twentieth centuries [DCN 102-108]; records of the various deans, including 'Dean Suckling's Book', diaries of Dean Prideaux, correspondence of Dean Pellew, and sermon notes of Dean Beeching [DCN 113-124].

Other series include records of peculiar jurisdiction [DCN 67-78]; records of precinct jurisdiction, including sessions rolls and coroner's inquests [DCN 79-83]; returns of scholars maintained at Trinity College and Gonville and Caius College, Cambridge, 1586-1683 [DCN 100]; records relating to eighteenth- and nineteenth-century Norwich charities [DCN 96-99]; and records of the cathedral school collected by Canon E. A. Parr [DCN 101]. There are a number of antiquarian papers, including two volumes of nineteenth-century drawings of the cathedral and four watercolours of 1830-2 painted by David Hodgson [DCN 125, 127]. Stored with the cathedral archives are a quantity of family and business records of the Thurlow, Kitson, Rackham and Bensly families, who acted as diocesan registrars or chapter clerks [DCN 126] and of the architect John Brown and his two sons, employed as cathedral surveyors [DCN 131].

Some manor court records among the cathedral archives continue into the late sixteenth and early seventeenth centuries [DCN 60], but most post-Reformation manor court records, together with plans of the chapter estates and many leases, passed into the hands of the Church Commissioners: these records are now on deposit in the Norfolk Record Office.

The inhabitants of the precinct were parishioners of the church of St Mary in the Marsh. The church itself was closed down in 1564 and the parishioners then used the chapel of St Luke in the Cathedral. The parish records of St Mary in the Marsh are now on deposit in the Norfolk Record

Office. Certain clergy and other persons, by special permission, used the Cathedral proper; their baptisms, marriages and burials were recorded in registers still held by the sacrist, but there is a transcript of the sacrist's marriage register, 1697-1754 in the Norfolk Studies Library in Norwich and cathedral marriages between 1754 and 1906 were recorded in the registers of St Mary in the Marsh. There are two lists in the cathedral archives of monumental inscriptions within the cathedral [DCN 112].

The method of storage and classification of medieval charters in the cathedral is described in B. Dodwell, *The Charters of Norwich Cathedral Priory,* Part One (Pipe Roll Society, new series, xl (1974)). The archives were re-organised in the late seventeenth and early eighteenth centuries by Dean Prideaux - many charters have annotations by him and he was probably responsible for the present numbering of the registers and for the binding up of documents into four *Libri Miscellaneorum.* The obedientiary rolls and early manor court rolls were numbered and described by Dr Saunders in the early twentieth century. Barbara Dodwell, as honorary cathedral archivist, numbered almost every document while the archives were still in the cathedral in a room over St Luke's chapel and she began the long process of sorting and classifying the records.

The library of Norwich Cathedral remains in the cathedral and is administered there by the vice-dean and custos.

A further deposit of cathedral archives (mainly nineteenth- and twentieth-century papers, with some antiquarian records), was made in 1996. These are listed as DCN 132-153.

DEAN AND CHAPTER RECORDS: CLASS LISTS

FINANCIAL RECORDS: OLD FOUNDATION

1. OBEDIENTIARY ROLLS

   - 1/1. MASTER OF THE CELLAR
   - 1/2, 3. CELLARER
   - 1/4. SACRIST
   - 1/5. CHAMBERLAIN
   - 1/6. ALMONER
   - 1/7. HOSTILAR
   - 1/8. REFECTORER
   - 1/9. PRECENTOR
   - 1/10. INFIRMAR
   - 1/11. GARDENER
   - 1/12. COMMUNAR AND PITANCER
   - 1/13. STATUS OBEDIENTIARORUM

2. DEPENDENT CELLS AND HOSPITAL

   - 2/1. LYNN
   - 2/2. ALDEBY
   - 2/3. ST LEONARD'S, THORPE
   - 2/4. YARMOUTH
   - 2/5. HOSPITAL OF ST PAUL, NORWICH
   - 2/6. HOXNE, SUFFOLK

3. INVENTORIES OF CELLS, MANORS, CARNARY CHAPEL

4. CHANTRIES, FOUNDATIONS AND ACCOUNTS

5. FIRST FRUITS

6. ECCLESIASTICAL TAXATION

7. LAY TAXATION: THE NINTH OF 1297

8. LAY TAXATION: FEUDAL AIDS

9. MISCELLANEOUS FINANCIAL RECORDS (INCLUDING ACCOUNT ROLL OF STEWARD OF GREAT HOSPITAL AND OF DEBTORS OF ROBERT TOPPES)

FINANCIAL RECORDS: NEW FOUNDATION

10. RECEIVER'S AND TREASURER'S ROLLS

11. AUDIT BOOKS

12. AUDIT PAPERS

13. RENT BOOKS

14. FINES ACCOUNTS

15. ANNUAL ACCOUNT SUMMARIES

16. DRAFT ACCOUNTS

17. DAY BOOKS

18. DEAN'S AND PREBENDARIES' ACCOUNTS

19. CAPITULAR ESTATE ACCOUNTS

20. PENSIONS AND PORTIONS ACCOUNTS

21. BANK BOOKS

22. OTHER VOLUMES OF ACCOUNTS, including timber and timber fund accounts residence repairs accounts

23. NEW FOUNDATION MISCELLANEOUS FINANCIAL RECORDS

THE CHAPTER

24. CHAPTER BOOKS

25. CHAPTER PAPERS

26. CHAPTER CLERK'S PAPERS

27. PRIVATE REGISTERS

28. THE STATUTES

29. LIBRI MISCELLANEORUM

CATHEDRAL OFFICIALS

30. CONGÉ D'ÉLIRE

31. GRANTS OF THE DEANERY

32. PRESENTATIONS TO PREBENDS

33. MINOR CANONRIES

34. MANDATES FOR INDUCTION

35. RESIGNATIONS, RENUNCIATIONS, ETC.

36. CATHEDRAL SUBSCRIPTION BOOK

37. TESTIMONIALS

38. MISCELLANEOUS PAPERS, OLD FOUNDATION

39. MISCELLANEOUS PAPERS, NEW FOUNDATION

DOCUMENTS OF TITLE

40. REGISTERS, CARTULARIES, INVENTORIES OF MUNIMENTS (including St Benet's cartulary)

41. ROYAL CHARTERS

42/1. ARCHIEPISCOPAL

42/2. PAPAL

43. EPISCOPAL

44. PRIVATE GRANTS, ETC.: NORFOLK AND OUT COUNTY

45. PRIVATE GRANTS, ETC.: NORWICH CITY

46. EAST ANGLIAN RELIGIOUS HOUSES

ESTATE LEASES

47. LEDGER BOOKS (i.e., lease registers)

47A. GENERAL LEASES OF DEAN GARDINER

48. ORIGINAL LEASES: NORWICH CITY

49. ORIGINAL LEASES: NORFOLK AND OUT COUNTY

50. TITHE RENT CHARGE PAPERS

ESTATE RENTALS AND SURVEYS

51. RENTALS AND SURVEYS NOT BOUND INTO VOLUMES

52. RENTALS AND SURVEYS IN VOLUME FORM

ESTATE PAPERS

53. INCLOSURE PAPERS

54. NAR VALLEY DRAINAGE

55. LYNN AND FAKENHAM RAILWAY

56. DILAPIDATIONS: HOUSES IN THE CLOSE

56A. DILAPIDATIONS: CANONRY HOUSES

57. ESTATE PAPERS: THE PRECINCT

58. ESTATE PAPERS: NORWICH CITY ESTATES

59. ESTATE PAPERS: COUNTY AND OUT COUNTY

MANORIAL RECORDS

60. MANOR COURT ROLLS AND BAILIFF'S ACCOUNT ROLLS BOXED BY MANOR

61. COURT AND ACCOUNT ROLLS NOT BOXED BY MANOR

61A. MISCELLANEOUS ITEMS RE COURTS

62. GROUPED MANOR ACCOUNTS

63. GROUPED MANOR COURT BOOKS, including BROMHOLME PRIORY

64. SHEEP ACCOUNTS

65. STEWARDS' MANORIAL ACCOUNTS

66. PROFITS OF MANORS AND ESTIMATIONS OF GRANGES

PECULIAR ADMINISTRATION

67. ACTA AND COMPERTA ROLLS

68. MARRIAGE LICENCE BONDS

69. REGISTER COPIES OF WILLS

70. ORIGINAL WILLS, including some non-probate wills acquired with title deeds

71. ADMINISTRATION ACT BOOKS

72. ADMINISTRATION BONDS

73. PROBATE INVENTORIES

74. CORONER'S INQUESTS

75. PENANCES AND RETRACTIONS

76. VISITATION RECORDS (visitations of its Peculiar by the Dean and Chapter)

77. ADMINISTRATIVE AND GENERAL PAPERS, including faculty book

77A. CONSOLIDATIONS, ETC. OF NORWICH PARISHES

78. OBLIGATIONS

PRECINCT JURISDICTION

79. HOLMSTREET LEET AND FAIR COURT

80. SHERIFF'S WARRANTS

81. SESSIONS ROLLS

82. SESSIONS PAPERS

83. ALEHOUSE LICENCES

LEGAL DOCUMENTS

84. ECCLESIASTICAL COURTS: COUNTY AND OUT COUNTY

85. ECCLESIASTICAL COURTS: NORWICH

86. CIVIL AND CRIMINAL COURTS

87. DISPUTES, AGREEMENTS: CARMELITES

88. DISPUTES, AGREEMENTS: CARROW

88A. DISPUTES, AGREEMENTS: ST MARY IN THE FIELDS

89. DISPUTES, AGREEMENTS BETWEEN CATHEDRAL AND CITY

90. LAWSUITS: COUNTY AND OUT COUNTY

91. LEGAL PAPERS: MISCELLANEOUS

EPISCOPAL AND DIOCESAN

92. BISHOP'S VISITATIONS OF THE CATHEDRAL

93. PATENT BOOKS

94. SEQUESTRATION BOOK AND CAVEAT BOOK

95. DIOCESAN MATERIAL AMONG CATHEDRAL ARCHIVES (including St Benet's)

CHARITIES, SCHOLARS AND SCHOOLS

96. PAYMENTS TO POOR AND MISCELLANEOUS PAPERS

97. NORRIS CHARITY

98. NORMAN AND SIMON CHARITIES

99. NORWICH CHARITY SCHOOLS

100. RETURNS OF SCHOLARS AT TRINITY AND AT GONVILLE AND CAIUS, CAMBRIDGE

101. CATHEDRAL CHOIR SCHOOL

THE CATHEDRAL FABRIC

102. SALVIN PAPERS

103. RESTORATION OF WEST FRONT

104. REPAIRS TO TOWER AND SPIRE

105. OTHER VICTORIAN WORK: BISHOP PELHAM MEMORIAL THRONE; ORGAN AND ORGAN CASE; RESTORATION OF CLOISTERS

106. WAR MEMORIAL CHAPEL

107. MISCELLANEOUS PAPERS RE. REPAIRS (including organ accounts 1607-1609, Cathedral repairs account 1660)

108. REPARATION, ORGAN AND VISITORS' FUND PAPERS

109. SERVICES: SERVICE REGISTER AND SPECIAL SERVICE FORMS

110. REGISTERS OF ATTENDANCE OF CANONS

111. CATHEDRAL INVENTORIES

112. CATHEDRAL MONUMENTAL INSCRIPTIONS

DEAN'S PERSONAL PAPERS

113. SUCKLING ('Dean Suckling's Book')

114. CROFTS

115. PRIDEAUX (diaries, antiquarian manuscripts)

116. COLE

117. BULLOCK

118. LLOYD

119. TURNER

120. PELLEW (diary, dean's notebook, correspondence)

121. GOULBURN

122. LEFROY

123. BEECHING

124. WILLINK

MISCELLANEOUS

125. ANTIQUARIAN

126. NON-CATHEDRAL RECORDS
    1. Thurlow family deeds and papers
    2. Solicitors papers, Kitson and Rackham
    3. Solicitors papers, Bensly and Bolingbroke
    4. Miscellaneous papers, no obvious connection to Cathedral

127. MAPS AND PLANS

128. WATER COLOURS BY DAVID HODGSON

129. SEAL MATRICES, ETC.

130. XEROXES OF DEAN AND CHAPTER RECORDS

131. PAPERS OF CATHEDRAL SURVEYORS

1996 DEPOSIT

132. LETTER BOOKS, 1888-1940.

133. FINANCIAL - CASH BOOKS AND LEDGERS, 1840-1950.

134. FINANCIAL - COLLECTIONS ACCOUNTS, 1900-60.

135. FINANCIAL - BANK BOOKS, 1882-1932.

136. FINANCIAL - INVOICES, 1986-87.

137. ESTATE PAPERS - THE CLOSE, 1803-1954.

138. ESTATE PAPERS - CITY ESTATES, 1824-48.

139. ESTATE PAPERS - COUNTRY ESTATES, 1870-1938.

140. CATHEDRAL VISITORS' BOOKS, 1885-1907.

141. SERVICE REGISTERS, 1920-84.

142. SPECIAL SERVICE FORMS, 1882, 1962-93.

143. SACRIST'S CORRESPONDENCE FILES, 1978-93.

144. SACRIST'S OFFICE DIARIES, 1953-93.

145. ANTIQUARIAN RECORDS.

146. LEGAL MEMORANDA, 1895-1934.

147. THE BOOK OF REMEMBRANCE.

148. CATHEDRAL REFERENCE BOOK.

149. WILLS OF THE DEAN AND MRS GOULBURN, *c.*1868-*c.*1889.

150. DIOCESAN AND EPISCOPAL, 1823-1941.

151. CONGÉ D' ÉLIRE, 1985.

152. SOLICITORS' PAPERS, 1802-1909.

153. PLANS, 1961.

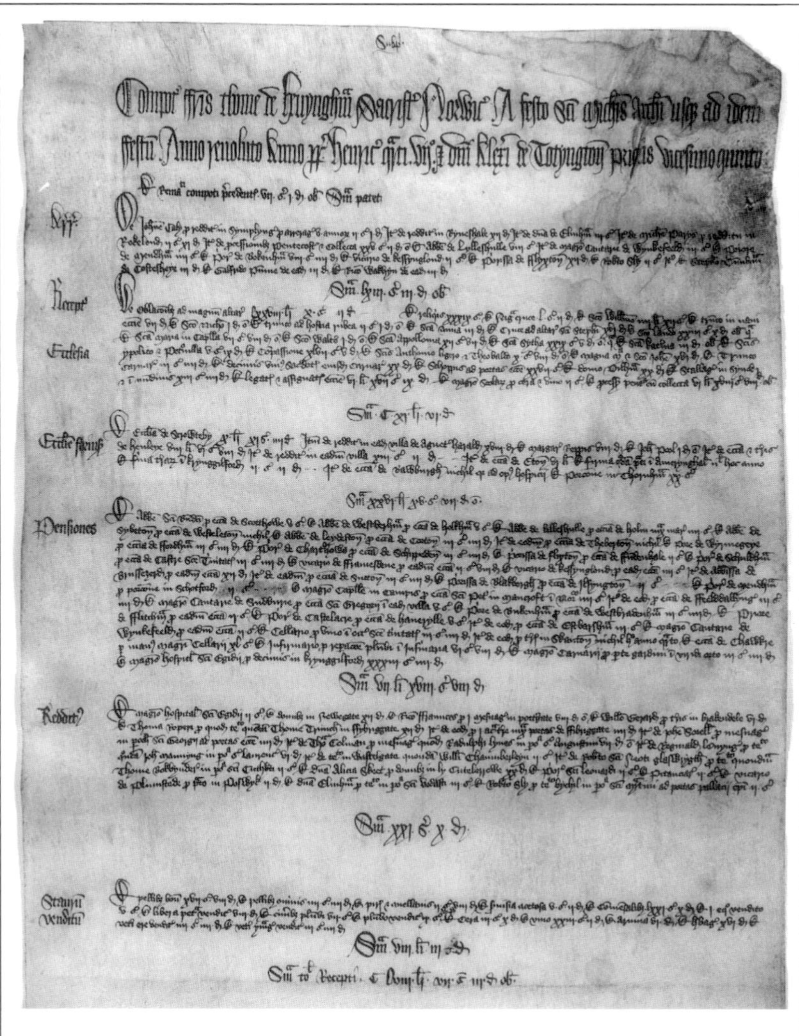

The Cathedral archive includes over 1,500 account rolls of the obedientiaries or officials of the medieval priory. This is the account roll for the sacrist for the year 1404 - 5. His income includes donations left at the High Altar and at the shrine of St William. *DCN 1/4/48*

FINANCIAL RECORDS: OLD FOUNDATION

DCN 1/ OBEDIENTIARY ROLLS

The records of the obedientiaries or officials of the various departments of the priory form a collection of about 1,500 rolls from the late thirteenth century to the Dissolution. Only one roll survives from before the time of William de Kirkeby, who became prior in 1272, following the riots in which parts of the precinct and documents of the priory were destroyed. The following list gives a summary account of the duties of each official and the estates from which their income derived. For more details of the content of the rolls, see H. W. Saunders, *An Introduction to the Obedientiary and Manor rolls of Norwich Cathedral Priory* (Norwich, 1930). Cartularies survive for the estates of several of the officials and these are noted below.

1. **MASTER OF THE CELLAR, 1263: 1272-1536 (110 rolls).**
The most important office, also referred to as the Prior's Department: the earliest rolls are headed 'CAMERA PRIORIS'. The department covers the expenses of the prior, including clothes and the entertaining of important guests, as well as activities of a cellarer including supply of bread and beer. Main income derives from the sixteen 'prior's manors' listed in the Introduction, as well as from many small estates in Norfolk, tenements in Norwich and churches of Sedgford, Fring, Hindringham, Elmham, Hindolveston, Sprowston, Hemsby, and of Westhall, Suffolk.
CARTULARY: DCN 40/1.

2, 3. **CELLARER, 1280-1531 (115 rolls).**
Control of the kitchen, apart from what the master of the cellar has taken over. Income from prior's manors, manors of Fring, Cressingham, Harpley, Hopton and Scampton, Lincs, rents from tenements in Norwich, estates in Hardingham and Hempstead, churches in Martham, Wighton, Wiggenhall, Hemblington, Hempstead, and Chalk in Kent.
CARTULARY: DCN 40/11.

4. **SACRIST, 1272-1536 (126 rolls).**
Maintenance of cathedral fabric and services. Expenditure normally listed under the heads of 'church' and 'vestry'. Includes expenses for building work including the campanile, 1291-1308, the clock, 1322, 1323. Receipts are from offerings at the various altars, from churches of Scratby, Eaton,

Bawburgh, Costessey and Henley, Suffolk, from rents on estates in Norwich, Braydeston, Fritton, Bawburgh, Cringleford, Ormesby, Scratby and Trowse.
CARTULARY: DCN 40/11

5. **CHAMBERLAIN, 1291-1536 (152 rolls).**
Clothing for monks. Income includes receipts from manors at Lakenham, Trowse, Arminghall, rents from estates in Norwich, Arminghall, Bracondale, Stoke Holy Cross, Barford and Lakenham.
CARTULARY: DCN 40/6.

6. **ALMONER, 1273-1533 (133 rolls).**
Primarily the distribution of charities. Income from manors and churches in Norwich, Wicklewood, Crownthorpe, Carrow, Strumpshaw and elsewhere.
CARTULARY: DCN 40/2/1.

7. **HOSTILAR, 1319-1535 (148 rolls).**
Equipment of the Guest Hall and attached chambers. Income from churches and tenements in Norwich.
NO CARTULARY.

8. **REFECTORER, 1288-1535 (119 rolls).**
Maintenance of and equipment for refectory; equipment of vessels for prior's department, infirmary and chamber for those being bled. Income from rents in Norwich.
NO CARTULARY.

9. **PRECENTOR, 1282-1533 (98 rolls).**
Duties related to services, to care of books, also a share in the clothing and physical comfort of the monks. Income from rents in Norwich, Plumstead and Kimberley.
NO CARTULARY.

10. **INFIRMAR, 1312-1530 (38 rolls).**
The care of the sick. Income from rents and churches in Norwich.
NO CARTULARY.

11. **GARDENER, 1329-1530 (34 rolls).**
The care of the gardens supplying fruit and produce for refectory and infirmary. Income from leasing portions of garden.
NO CARTULARY.

12. **COMMUNAR AND PITANCER, 1282-1536 (112 rolls).**
From the names, these officials might be expected to look after the commons or ordinary rations and pitances or delicaces. In fact, the main expenditure is for building work, including the cloisters and chapter house. Smaller expenses include travelling expenses for priory officials, gifts, and support for scholars at Oxford. Receipts for the communar come mainly from the church at Catton: the pitancer has various small rents and also income from the cellarer.

13. **STATUS OBEDIENTIARUM, 1363-1534 (7 rolls).**
Totals of income and expenditure from the various departments. Survive for seven years only.

DCN 2/ THE DEPENDENT CELLS

The priory had small dependent cells at St Leonard's in Thorpe, Lynn, Aldeby, Yarmouth, and Hoxne, Suffolk: no account rolls survive for any of them before the mid-fourteenth century. In addition, the priory administered the hospital of St Paul, Norwich.

1. **LYNN, 1370-1536 (71 rolls).**
Income derives from land and rents in Lynn, Gaywood, Bawsey, Outwell and Upwell, Mintlyn, Wiggenhall and Middleton: and the church of St Margaret, the chapels of St James and St Nicholas, and the gild of Holy Trinity, all in Lynn.

2. **ALDEBY, 1380-1526 (30 rolls).**
Income from offerings, lands and tithes in Aldeby.

3. **ST LEONARD'S, THORPE, 1348-1536 (140 rolls).**
Income from offerings at St Leonard's, chapel of St Michael, Thorpe; rents from lands in Norwich, Thorpe, Pockthorpe, and Taverham. As well as expenses on the cell, St Leonard's made an annual payment of one or two shillings to each monk in the cathedral community.

4. **YARMOUTH, 1355-1529 (21 rolls).**
Income from the chapel of St Mary, Yarmouth, and also from land at Thurlton.

5. **HOSPITAL OF ST PAUL, NORWICH, 1422-1510 (7 rolls).** Receipts are described under three headings: rents; tithes and portions; corrodies. The rents were mainly from properties in St Paul's parish, Norwich, with some from other parishes in the city; the tithes were from the parish of Ormesby. A small sum came from the manor of Normans (the hospital of St Paul is often known as Normanspital after its first master). With the accounts is a roll describing the constitutions of the Hospital.

6. **HOXNE, 1394-1535 (45 rolls).** Receipts came from Hoxne, tithes in Syleham, South Elmham, Denham, and the manor of Yaxley, all in Suffolk.

DCN 3/ INVENTORIES

1. Inventory of prior's manors: covers Plumstead, Elmham, Eaton, Hemsby, Newton, Sedgeford, Gnatingdon, Thornham, Hindringham, Hindolveston, Taverham. Records furniture, farming implements, etc. Newton and Sedgeford inventories are dated 1352.

2. Inventory of vestments, *c.*1470.

3. Inventory of cell at Yarmouth, *c.*1480.

4. Inventory of the carnary chapel, Norwich, 1481.

5. Valuation of utensils, etc. at Taverham, 15th-16th centuries.

DCN 4/ CHANTRIES

1. Agreement re chantry established by Letitia Payne in St Stephen and St Peter Mancroft churches in Norwich, 1316. (For related title deeds see DCN 45/39).

2. *Inspeximus* by priory of letter patent re chaplain of Mendlesham, Suffolk, 1331.

3. Fragments only of instrument by prior William Claxton, relating to masses for souls of Bishop Herbert and others, 1335.

4. Letters patent for establishment of chantry at Hellesdon by John Churchman, 1394.

5. Agreement re provision of masses for Bishop John Wakering, 1427.

6. Agreement re establishment of chantry in the Cathedral by Elizabeth Clere, 1478.

7-10. Accounts for chantries of John Wakering, Thomas Erpingham and Robert Ty in the Cathedral, 1457-85 (four years only).

DCN 5-8 ECCLESIASTICAL AND LAY TAXATION

5. ECCLESIASTICAL TAXATION: FIRST FRUITS; including attestation re first fruits, *temp.* Bishop Salmon [1299-1325]; collectors' accounts for Archdeaconries of Sudbury and Suffolk, 1460-1, 1466-7, and for Archdeaconries of Norfolk and Norwich, 1465-6.

6. ECCLESIASTICAL TAXATION: documents relating to collections of tenths in Norwich diocese, 1315-1427.

7. LAY TAXATION: assessment rolls for the ninth of 1297 of six parishes in Clackclose hundred and seven parishes in Freebridge Lynn hundred.

8. LAY TAXATION: book of feudal aids covering seventeen hundreds in Norfolk [probably 1346-7].

DCN 9 MISCELLANEOUS FINANCIAL RECORDS, 1213-1515

Including granary accounts, 1268-9, 1384-5; receiver's account of Robert Cresswell as steward of Great Hospital, Norwich [1520-1]; account roll of debtors of Robert Toppes, alderman of Norwich, apparently drawn up at his death in 1467.

FINANCIAL RECORDS: NEW FOUNDATION

Post-Reformation financial records survive in several forms. Receiver's accounts in roll form exist, 1538-1677, the earliest being accounts of individual prebendaries rather than overall accounts. Receiver's accounts for 1538, 1622 and 1630 are bound into DCN 29/3. Treasurer's rolls survive from 1622. There are working accounts for the receiver and treasurer for 1619-46 and 1661-79 and formal audit books from 1660 onwards. Audit accounts survive for two years before 1660: those for 1538 are bound in the first volume of working accounts [DCN 10/2/1] and those for 1638 in the first audit book [DCN 11/1]. Supporting audit papers survive in small numbers from the mid-sixteenth century and for most years between 1613-32 and from 1685 onward: they are arranged in yearly bundles. There are several series of subsidiary accounts, listed below.

DCN 10/ RECEIVER'S AND TREASURER'S ACCOUNTS

1. Receiver's rolls, 1538-1687, treasurer's rolls, 1622-87.

2. Receiver's and treasurer's accounts, 1619-46, 1661-79. Receipts and payments for 1580 are bound into DCN 10/2/1.

DCN 11 Audit books, 1660-1902. Receipts and payments for 1638 are bound into DCN 11/1.

DCN 12 Audit papers, *c.*1557-20th century (many gaps in early period).

DCN 13 Rent accounts, 1683-1901.

DCN 14 Fines accounts, 1817-68.

DCN 15 Annual account summaries, 1812-48.

DCN 16 Draft accounts, 1849-1924.

DCN 17 Day books, 1821-1919.

DCN 18 Dean's and Prebendaries' accounts, 1758-1901.

DCN 19 Capitular estates accounts, 1859-69.

DCN 20 Pensions and portions accounts, 1722-1849.

DCN 21 Bank books, 1811-60.

DCN 22 Other volumes of accounts include extraordinary expenses, 1798-1874 and timber fund accounts, 1779-1842.

DCN 23 Miscellaneous financial papers, *c.*1557-1936, including summary account of fines 1800-30; notes re sale of timber, 1794-1828.

THE CHAPTER

The dean and chapter was founded by Henry VIII in 1538 and refounded by Edward VI in 1547. The earliest surviving chapter act book begins in 1566 and the series is complete from that date (there was no chapter between 1649 and 1660). Supporting chapter papers and chapter clerk's papers survive from the eighteenth century.

At times, books have also been kept containing a more detailed record of chapter business than is recorded in the act books:

1694-1724, in Dean Prideaux's diaries [DCN 115/1-3].
1829-66, in Dean Pellew's diaries [DCN 120/1-7].
1870-84, in the Private Registers [DCN 27/3, 4].
1886-89, in Dean Goulburn's notebooks [DCN 121/5-8].

DCN 24/ CHAPTER ACT BOOKS

1.	1566-1614.
2.	1614-49.
3.	1660-91.
4.	1691-1732.
5.	1733-94.
6.	1795-1833.
7.	1834-56.
8.	1857-78.
9.	1878-88.
10.	1888-97.
11.	1897-1914.
12.	1915-39.
13.	Abridgement of chapter book entries, 1566-1660.
14-16.	Indexes to chapter books, 1888-1939.

DCN 25 CHAPTER PAPERS

Supporting papers, 1693-1947.

DCN 26 CHAPTER CLERK'S PAPERS

Supporting papers, including accounts, 1773-1811, correspondence, 1850-87, papers re cathedral fabric repair fund, *c.*1870-1922, record of seal fees paid, 1823-1923.

DCN 27/ PRIVATE REGISTERS

These contain two distinct forms of record. The first three volumes are a consequence of the chapter resolution of 28 November 1682 to have a register in which could be entered details of leases, rents and fines. This was carried back to 1660 in summary form. These registers were discontinued in 1829: from 1870, the same volumes were used for a detailed record of chapter meetings.

1. 1660-1743 (lease register).
2. 1744-1828 (lease register).
3. 1828-29 (lease register) and 1870-79 (chapter meetings).
4. 1880-84 (chapter meetings).

DCN 28 STATUTES

An undated set of statutes copied from a mutilated original is bound into DCN 29/2: these are probably the Henrician statutes, no other copy of which exists in Norwich. What seem to be statutes of Elizabeth I for Norwich are in the British Library (Stowe MS 128): there is no copy in Norwich. Statutes were issued by James I in 1620 and the Cathedral was governed by these from then on. New statutes have been issued in 1941 and 1966.

DCN 29/ LIBRI MISCELLANEORUM

Four volumes of documents, mostly of the sixteenth and seventeenth centuries, probably collected together by Dean Prideaux. Some of the more important items are:

1. Valuation of cathedral estates, *c.*1538; record of visitation of Cathedral by commission appointed by Elizabeth I, 1568; statutes of James I; scheme of state of church when resigned into hands of Elizabeth I, 1587.

2. History of cathedral and its liberties; statutes, apparently of Henry VIII; foundation charters of Henry VIII and Edward VI; letter of Archbishop Laud re cathedral appointments, 1634; papers re dispute over Yarmouth church, 17th century.

3. Manorial accounts for prior's manors for seven years between 1510 and 1535; receiver's accounts, 1538, 1622, 1630.

4. Copy of agreement between city of Norwich and the Cathedral upon award of Cardinal Wolsey, 1524; statutes of James I; lease of Close made by the city in 1655; contributions and disbursements for cathedral repairs at the Restoration; report by attorney-general re right of the Cathedral to pensions out of the Exchequer, 1706.

CATHEDRAL OFFICIALS

For the pre-Reformation period, records of cathedral officials are primarily to be found in the obedientiary rolls, records of dependent cells and bailiffs' accounts. Subsequently, the main records are the appointments recorded in the Chapter Act books and the payment of salaries recorded in the treasurer's rolls and audit books.

By charter of 2 May 1538 Henry VIII created the dean and chapter, comprising six prebends: the nomination to these offices was reserved to the Crown, exercised by the Lord Chancellor. By the Cathedral Act of 3 and 4 Victoria *cap.*113 [11 August 1840] all residentiary members of the chapter, except the dean, were styled canons: at the time, the second and third canons were suspended, so that after that date there are only four canons. By letters patent of Queen Anne dated 26 April 1714, the first prebend that fell vacant was to be annexed forever to the Mastership of St Catherine's College, Cambridge. The first to fall vacant was the fourth prebend in 1719 and this was annexed accordingly. This arrangement continued until 1927.

DCN 30 Congés d'Élire, 1676-1910.

DCN 31 Grants of the deanery, 1790-1952.

DCN 32 Presentations to prebends, 1570-1951.

DCN 33 Appointments and other papers relating to minor canons, 1701-1841.

DCN 34 Mandates for induction, 1886-1926.

DCN 35 Resignations, renunciations, appointments to livings, 1303-1507, 1543-1762.

DCN 36 Cathedral officials' subscription book, 1750-1811.

DCN 37 Testimonials, 1713-29.

DCN 38 Appointments of officials: old foundation, 1395-1531 [5 documents only].

DCN 39 Appointments of officials: new foundation with related papers, including precentors' or chanters' books, 1629-38, book of appointments and dismissals of choristers, 1785-1829, lists of officials, *c.*1821-*c.*1938.

DOCUMENTS OF TITLE

The earliest surviving records of Norwich Cathedral are royal, episcopal and private grants to the priory from the time of its establishment in Norwich in *c.*1095, with one royal charter addressed to the Bishop of Thetford predating the move. The medieval arrangement of these documents is shown in the inventory of muniments [DCN 40/12] and by pressmarks on the documents themselves:

A, B.	royal grants issued to the priory.
C.	royal grants pertaining to the bishopric.
D-F.	episcopal charters.
G.	final concords.
J-Z.	private grants arranged topographically and by official.

The possessions of the infirmarer, pitancer and hostilar are included under the villages in which they also had estates. The inventory does not include records of the possessions of the almoner, chamberlain or refectorer nor of the dependent cells. Papal bulls and the acta of archbishops are also omitted, although papal mandates for particular churches are included as title for those churches.

A large number of grants are transcribed into cartularies (known usually as registers), normally without witness or dating clauses. There is no overall cartulary for the priory, but there are cartularies for the larger departments: master of the cellar, almoner, cellarer, chamberlain and sacrist.

DCN 40/ REGISTERS, CARTULARIES, INVENTORIES OF MUNIMENTS

The cathedral cartularies are known as 'registers': there is no overall cartulary, but DCN 40/1 includes royal, episcopal and papal grants as well as title deeds for the prior's manors. Three items have been stored with the registers for a long time and became known as registers too: the St Benet's cartulary [DCN 40/8], the letter book [DCN 40/9] and the record of profits of manors [DCN 40/13].

1. **REGISTRUM PRIMUM** [Davis, *Medieval Cartularies of Great Britain* (1958), entry no. 702]. Early 14th century. Begins with chronicle incorporating royal and episcopal grants. Followed by royal charters,

papal bulls and final concords, then topographical section dealing with prior's manors (covering Sedgeford, Thornham, Hindringham, Hindolveston, Taverham, Elmham, Gateley, Eaton, Keswick, Trowse Newton, Rockland, Surlingham, Sprowston, Catton, Pockthorpe, Plumstead, Postwick, Hemsby, Scratby, Ormesby, Martham and Denham in Suffolk). With episcopal charters of Bishop John Salmon, [1299-1325] and late 14th- and 15th- century miscellanea.

2. **REGISTRUM SECUNDUM.** Two distinct volumes long bound together, but now separated again.
DCN 40/2/1 [Davis, 711]. Almoner's Register. Estates in Norwich, Attlebridge, Wicklewood, 13th-14th centuries.
DCN 40/2/2 [Davis, 703]. An incomplete copy of DCN 40/1, 14th century.

3. **REGISTER OF ROYAL ACTA** [Davis, 706]. Compiled *c.*1500. Begins with a narrative, which increasingly becomes a collection of charters. Followed by list of city officials, 1399-1451, with occasional annals, then sections of royal charters to the priory and to the bishop.

4. **REGISTER OF EPISCOPAL GRANTS** [Davis, 705]. Compiled 15th century. Begins with priory's rights in the city of Norwich in the form of a chronicle: this is also found in the Norwich City Book of Pleas and in the Binham cartulary; followed by episcopal grants.

5. **CELLARER'S REGISTER** [Davis, 710]. Begun 1282, most entries 14th and 15th century. Begins with a small group of royal and episcopal charters, followed by grants relating to tithes, then to temporal possessions of cellarer. Also contains much miscellaneous material of 14th and 15th centuries.

6. **CHAMBERLAIN'S REGISTER** [Davis, 709]. Compiled in three stages in 14th century. Chamberlain's holdings were mainly in Norwich, Stoke, Trowse, Arminghall. Also contains documents re Carrow convent and St Giles's Hospital, Norwich, with much later miscellanea.

7. **REGISTRUM SEPTUM** [Davis, 704]. Documents of general interest to the house begining with Bishop Herbert's foundation and Pope Paschal's confirmation, followed by royal charters, episcopal charters (arranged topographically, not by bishop), final concords, topographical section relating to Sedgeford and Thornham only, 13th-14th centuries.

8. **CARTULARY OF ABBEY OF ST BENET** [Davis, 498]. Late 14th century.

9. **LETTER BOOK** [Davis, 713]. Early 14th century. 63 folios, many of the letters are numbered, but this numbering is now out of sequence. Many lack a dating clause, those dated appear to be 1318-25.

10. **REGISTER OF ACTA** [Davis, 714]. 14th century. *Acta* of priors: dated instruments cover the period 1334-70.

11. **SACRIST'S REGISTER** [Davis, 712]. Late 13th century and later. Calendar, memoranda re work of sacrist, topographical section mixed with much miscellanea.

12. **INVENTORY OF MUNIMENTS** [Davis, 708]. Early 14th century. Lists muniments by type and private deeds by place.

DCN 41/ ROYAL CHARTERS: SUMMARY LIST

Early royal charters were arranged in two series: those relating to the priory and those pertaining to the bishopric. This order has been retained here. Later charters are listed in date order.

RELATING TO PRIORY

WILLIAM II

1. Grant of land in St Michael's, Norwich and in Taverham, [*c.*1096].

HENRY II

2. Confirmation to the monks of the church of St John at the castle gate in Norwich, [*c.*1162].

JOHN

3. Confirmation of liberties, 1200.
4. *Inspeximus* of charters of Bishop John de Grey, 1205

HENRY III

5. Confirmation that bishop and prior have amercements of tenants in fee, 1232.

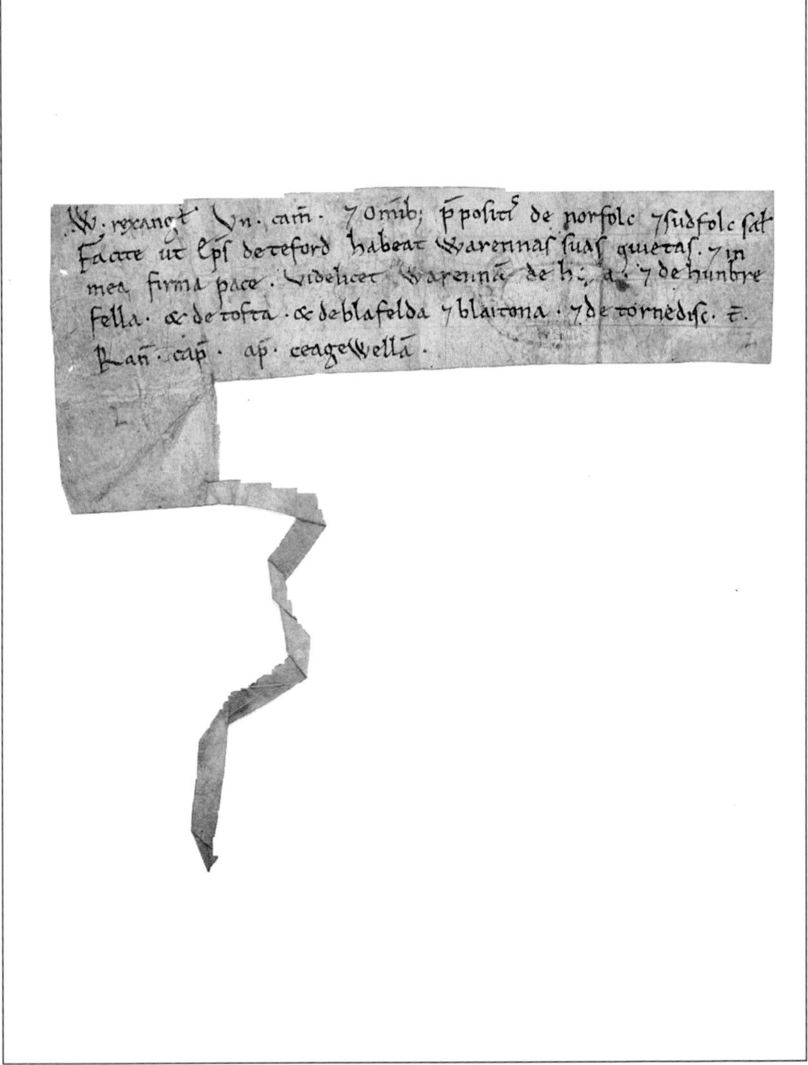

W. rex angl' Vn. cam. 7 omnib; ppositis de norfolc 7 sudfolc sal.
Facite ut Eps de teford habeat warennas suas quietas. 7 in
mea firma pace. Videlicet warenna de h.. a. 7 de hunbre
fella. & de tosta. & de blafelda 7 blaitona. 7 de tornedisc. T.
Ran. cap. ap. ceagewella.

Charter of William II to the Bishop of Thetford. This is the earliest document in the Cathedral archive and predates the move of the see to Norwich in 1096.
DCN 41/16

6. Confirmation of charter of Henry I re manor of Eaton and fairs in Norwich, Lynn and Hoxne, 1232.
7. Confirmation that prior and convent have free warren in their lands in Sedgeford, Hindolveston, Beckham, Plumstead, Gateley, Hemsby, Martham, Taverham, Newton, Eaton, Arminghall and Lakenham, 1248.

EDWARD I

8. Licence for alienation in mortmain of lands in Thornham, Martham, Sedgeford, Trowse, Hemsby, Hindolveston and Dilham, 1286.
9-11. Three copies of *inspeximus* of six earlier charters, 1306.
12. Two counterparts, formerly tied together, of *inspeximus* of royal charters re grants to hospital of St Paul, Norwich, 1306.
13. *Inspeximus* of agreement between priory and city of Norwich, 1306.
14. Licence for alienation in mortmain of messuages in St Vedast and St Michael at Plea, Norwich, 1293.
15. Pardon to the prior for entering, contrary to the statute of mortmain, into lands in Thurlton, 1300.

RELATING TO BISHOPRIC

WILLIAM II

16. Confirmation that bishop of Thetford has right of warren in Hoxne, Homersfield, Tofts [unidentified], Blofield, Beighton, Thornage, [1091 x 5].

HENRY III

17. Charter re collection of the tenth in the diocese of Norwich, 1289.
18. Grant to Holy Trinity and Bishop Thomas of the manor of Wykes [Ipswich, Suffolk], 1231.
19. Notification of quitclaim by the Bishop of Norwich for money due for the escape of Roger, son of John de Dunwich, clerk, from his prison at North Elmham, 1270.

EDWARD I

20. Licence for the bishop to acquire half a mill in Thornage, 1291.
21. Licence for the bishop of Norwich to acquire service of one knight's fee in Witnesham, Dagworth, Caldecote, Henley (all in Suffolk), 1285.
22. Licence for the bishop of Norwich to acquire service of one knight's fee as in DCN 41/21 and also of a half fee in Colne Engaine (Essex), 1286.

CHARTERS NOT INCLUDED IN THE INVENTORY

EDWARD I

23. Confirmation of rights of priory in Newgate and Holmstreet, Norwich, 1280.
24. Copy of grant of land in Ormesby, 1300.

EDWARD II

25. Copy of commission to enquire into dispute between priory and city re Tombland and Raton Rowe, Norwich, 1309.
26. Licence for alienation in mortmain of land in Morston, Aldeby, Sedgeford, Trowse Newton, Arminghall, Yarmouth, and Thorpe next Haddiscoe, 1316.
27, 28. Two copies of exemplification and confirmation of charters of predecessors, 1311.
29. Licence for alienation in mortmain of land in Hindringham, 1313.
30. Licence for alienation in mortmain of land in Trowse Newton, Norwich, Arminghall, Stoke Holy Cross and Hindolveston, 1314.
31. Two copies of licence for alienation in mortmain of advowson of church of Westhall (Suffolk), 1315.
32. Licence for alienation in mortmain of land in Sedgeford and Thurlton, 1325.
33. Licence for alienation in mortmain of land in Great Cressingham, Little Cressingham and Hopton (Suffolk), 1316.
34. Licence for alienation in mortmain of lands in Trowse Newton, Hindolveston, Stoke Holy Cross and Hoxne (Suffolk), 1318.
35 Licence for alienation in mortmain of land in Thurlton, 1320.
36. Licence for alienation in mortmain of land in Wood Norton, Henley (Suffolk), Attlebridge, Great Plumstead, Trowse Newton, Norwich, Hindringham, Catton, Hellesdon, Thurlton, Haddiscoe and Thorpe next Haddiscoe, 1325.
37. Writ in case of novel disseisin between priory and John Kempe concerning tenement in Norwich, 1325.
38. Writ concerning bishops' churches during episcopal vacancy, 1326.
39. Copy of licence for alienation in mortmain issued by Thomas, Marshal of England, of land in Trowse Newton, [1306x1338, ?1337-38].
40. Licence for alienation in mortmain of church of Chalk (Kent), 1327.
41. Licence for bishop to crenellate palace in Norwich and manses on his manors, 1327.

42. Licence for alienation in mortmain of lands in Morston, Aldeby, Sedgeford, Trowse Newton, Arminghall, Yarmouth, and Thorpe next Haddiscoe, 1330.

43. Licence for alienation in mortmain of three messuages in Norwich, 1331.

44. Notification that towns of Freckenham and Isleham are in diocese of Norwich, archdeaconry of Sudbury, deanery of Fordham, 1335.

45. Licence for alienation in mortmain of advowsons of church of Ryston and moiety of church of Fordham, 1336.

46. Licence for alienation in mortmain of lands in Martham, Whitlingham, Kirby Bedon, Trowse Newton, Thorpe, and Wood Norton, 1337.

47, 48. Two counterparts of exemplification and confirmation of earlier charters, 1338.

49. Licence for alienation in mortmain of land in Thurlton, Haddiscoe, Thorpe next Haddiscoe, Raveningham, Norton Subcourse, Yarmouth, Sedgeford and Hindolveston, 1340.

50. Two counterparts of exemplification of grant of corrody of John de Stretford, 1340.

51, 52. Charters re land of prior in Aldeby and Ormesby [which is] in the hands of the king's escheator, 1341.

53. Licence for alienation in mortmain of land in Thurlton, Haddiscoe, Thorpe next Haddiscoe, Raveningham, Norton Subcourse, Yarmouth, Sedgeford and Hindolveston, 1342.

54. Licence for alienation in mortmain of land in Pockthorpe, Norwich, Wood Norton, Sedgeford, Trowse, Wicklewood, Crownthorpe and Aldeby, 1346.

55. Letter patent concerning corrody of John de Stretford now dead, 1347.

56. Licence for alienation in mortmain of advowson of Fring, 1331.

57, 58. Two copies of *inspeximus* of plea made before the king concerning bridge at Lakenham, 1353.

59, 60. Two copies of licence for alienation in mortmain of land in Thurlton, Haddiscoe, Thorpe next Haddiscoe, Raveningham, Toft Monks and Lynn, 1356.

61. Licence for alienation in mortmain of land in Norwich, North Elmham, Hindolveston, Scratby, Hoxne (Suffolk), Denham (Suffolk), Attlebridge, Trowse and Wicklewood, 1358.

62. Licence for alienation in mortmain of advowson of church of Sprowston, 1361.

63. Licence for alienation in mortmain of land in Haddiscoe, Thorpe next Haddiscoe, Toft Monks and Thurlton; the priory to make annual distribution to the poor at Yarmouth, 1369.

64. Royal charter that prior and convent accept protection for one year, 1370.
65. Licence for alienation in mortmain of land in Bawburgh, Costessey, Great Melton, Wicklewood, Hoxne (Suffolk) and Denham (Suffolk), 1371.
66 Fragment of royal writ, [1371-72].

RICHARD II

67. Licence for alienation in mortmain of land in Lakenham, Trowse Newton, Bracondale, Lynn, Norwich, Yarmouth, Thurlton, Toft Monks, Thorpe next Haddiscoe, Raveningham, Thorpe next Norwich and Ormesby, 1392.
68. Writ to bishop H[enry de Spenser] re plea of transgression against the royal peace, 1397.

HENRY V

69. Licence for alienation in mortmain of land in Thurlton, Raveningham, Yarmouth, Scratby and Caister Holy Trinity, 1413.

HENRY VI

70. Confirmation of liberties, 1425.
71. Confirmation of charters of predecessors, 1428.
72. Confirmation to priory of advowson of Sprowston, 1429.
73. Confirmation of liberties in Holmstreet, 1438.
74. *Inspeximus* of inquisition confirming priory's rights in Newgate, Holmstreet, and the area anciently called Thedwardescroft in Norwich, 1441.
75, 76. Two counterparts of *inspeximus* and confirmation of royal charter of 7 May 1232, 1441.
77. Writ pardoning prior for keeping money of John Hancock, suicide, disputed between priory and mayor of Norwich, 1444.
78. Confirmation of grants of predecessors, 1445.
79. General pardon to prior and convent for all transgressions, 1446.
80. *Inspeximus* and confirmation of charter of 14 May 1347, re corrody of John de Stretford and grant that priory be not bound to grant any corrodies thereafter, 1447.
81. General pardon to Elizabeth Clere [benefactor to the priory], 1452.
82. General pardon to prior and convent [for all transgressions], 1455.

EDWARD IV

83. *Inspeximus* and confirmation of earlier charters, 1474.
84. Licence for alienation in mortmain of annual rents from manors of Claydon (Suffolk) and Tharston, 1478.
85. *Inspeximus* of entry in plea roll *de banco* re manors of Tharston and Claydon, 1480.
86. Grant to priory that it shall not be charged with further corrodies, 1482.

HENRY VII

87. Exemplification of petition of prior and convent concerning corrodies, 1488.
88. *Inspeximus* of entry in exchequer plea rolls re annual rent from St Paul's Hospital, Norwich, January 1496.

HENRY VIII

89. General pardon to prior and convent [for all transgressions], 1509.
90-92. Three counterparts of charter inspecting and confirming grants of predecessors, 1510.
93, 94. Two copies of writ concerning agreement between priory and city re priory's rights in Pentecost fair, Tombland, Holmstreet, Spitland, Raton Row, all in Norwich, 1521.
95. Licence for city to acquire lands and rents worth 20 marks per annum, 1524.
96. Licence for city to grant to prior 20 marks annual rent, 1524.
97. *Inspeximus* of plea roll *de banco* re rents disputed between priory and Hospital of St Giles, Norwich, 1534.
98. Form of letters patent for which priory petitions Henry VIII, [*c.*1525].
99. Composition between priory and city made through arbitration of Cardinal Wolsey, 1525.
100. Tripartite agreement between Queen Katherine, the mayor and community of Norwich, and priory re land in Field Dalling held of the honour of Clare, 1526.
101. Copy of writ re priory liberties in Norwich, 10 February 1537.
102. Foundation charter of Henry VIII, translating prior and convent into dean and chapter, 1538.
103. Letters patent declaring site of dean and chapter to be part of county of the city of Norwich and not of the county of Norfolk and hundred of Blofield, 1539.
104. Copy of writ re enquiry concerning St Peter Hungate church, Norwich, 1538.
105. *Inspeximus* of record of Court of Augmentations re grant to priory by Robert, abbot of Kirstead, of annual rent or pension arising from lands in Skampton and Thorpe, Lincs., 1541.

EDWARD VI

106. Foundation charter of Edward VI, 1547.
107. Charter and donation of Edward VI, 1547.
108. Copy of writ by John, bishop of Thetford, being the surrender of the dean and chapter into the hands of Edward VI (incomplete).

ELIZABETH I

109. Confirmation of donation charter of Edward VI, 1569.
110. Writ re tithes of Ringland rectory, 1581.
111. Copy of assignment by Elizabeth I to Henry Ryce of cathedral properties in Norfolk leased to Elizabeth by Dean Gardiner, 1588.
112. Copy of writ concerning money owed to Elizabeth I by dean and chapter, 1595.
113. Writ [to dean and chapter] concerning money owed to Elizabeth I, 1602.

JAMES I

114. Letters patent ordering commission to be set up to enquire into payment of fifteenths to the king from inhabitants of Holmstreet, Norwich, 1605.
115. Grant that chief steward and his deputy, dean, subdean, receiver or treasurer, and chief coroner may be justices of the peace within the precincts, 1610.
116. Statutes issued to the dean and chapter by James I, 1620.
117. *Inspeximus* of plea before king's court concerning a disputed messuage in Norwich, 1617.

CHARLES I

118. Copy of royal charter re interrogations in suit between dean and chapter and Nicholas Geff, 1626.
119. Charter determining period of residence of prebends, 1629.
120. Licence for alienation in mortmain of chapel of Wighton, 1635.
121. Grant to clergy of Norwich of a rate in lieu of tithes, 1638.

CHARLES II

122. Confirmation of charter of James I concerning justices of the peace within the precincts, 1660.
123. Confirmation of foundation charter of Edward VI, 1665.
124. Commission of gaol delivery for cathedral liberty, 1666.
125. Letter patent ordering John Duvall to pay arrears of rent due from Fring rectory, 1683.

ANNE

126. Confirmation of foundation charter of Edward VI, 1704.

GEORGE II

127. Charter establishing charity for relief of widows and children of clergymen, the Dean and Chapter to be on the governing body, 1741

UNDATED

128. *Inspeximus* of entry in plea roll concerning one quarter to a knight's fee in Aldeby held by William de Morley and prior of Holy Trinity, 7 Henry [probably 1419].

LATE COPIES

129. Copy of charters of 32 Henry III and 35 Edward I.
130. Fifteenth-century copy of grant by King Stephen to St Paul's Hospital, Norwich, of property in Norwich and Ormesby.

DCN 42/ ARCHIEPISCOPAL INSTRUMENTS

[nos. 1, 2, 3, 6 fully transcribed in DODWELL]

1. Archbishop T: confirmation to priory of church of St Giles in Norwich, [probably Archbishop Theobold, 1139-61].

2. Archbishop Hubert: composition between bishop and priory re church at Martham, [1195-98].

3. Archbishop John: confirmation of churches, chapels and cells, 1281.

4. Henry, prior of Canterbury: *inspeximus* of earlier charters, 1302.

5-8. Archbishop Robert: injunctions at visitation and related documents, 1304-06.

9. Archbishop Walter Reynolds: *inspeximus* of charter of Bishop John Salmon establishing chapel, 1316.

10-15 Compositions between Archbishop Simon and prior of Norwich re spiritual jurisdiction, the see of Norwich being vacant, 1330.

16. Commission for visitation by Archbishop John to prior of Bodnash, 1336.

17, 18. Archbishop Simon: confirmation of exchange between priory and the bishopric of Norwich, in which the priory gives church of Chalk in Kent for manor of Cobham College in Martham, 1380, with publication of bull of Pope Urban VI re the exchange, 1383.

DCN 43/ EPISCOPAL CHARTERS

HERBERT LOSINGA

1. Grant of manor of Fring, [1109-19].

EVERARD

2. Confirmation of agreement re lands at Bacton, [1121-35].
3. Grant of lands in Beckham, Hempstead, Plumstead, service of Ralph of Thorpe, tithes in Cressingham, Sedgeford, Elmham and in Homersfield, Suffolk, [?1141-43].

WILLIAM TURBE

4. General confirmation of previous grants, [1146-47].
5. Grant of church of Scratby, [1160-70].

JOHN OF OXFORD

6. Grant to the church of St Margaret, Lynn of the chapel of St Nicholas, [1186-1200].
7. Grant to Ralph of Hindolveston of tithes of Langham, excepting pensions to Norwich priory and St Paul's Hospital, Norwich, [1186-1200].
8. Confirmation of appropriation to priory of church of St Saviour, Norwich, [1186-1200].

JOHN DE GRAY

9. Grant of indulgence for contributions to work of hospital of St Paul, 1201.
10. Grant of church of St Margaret, Ormesby to work of hospital of St Paul, 1205.
11. Appropriation of church of St Andrew, Eaton to office of sacrist, 1205.
12. Appropriation of church of All Saints, Scratby to office of sacrist, 1205.

13-15. Agreement between bishop and priory for exchange of Lynn market and manor of Sedgeford, with appropriation of church of Sedgeford to office of cellarer, 1205.

16, 17. Counterparts of appropriation of church of Wighton to the office of cellarer, 1205.

18. Appropriation of church of St Margaret, Lynn, chapels of St James and St Nicholas, Lynn, church of Mintlynn, tithes from demesne of Gaywood, 1205.

19. Exchange between bishop and priory of rights in Lynn for Sedgeford and Cressingham manors, 1205.

20. Agreement between bishop and priory re churches of Sedgeford, Witton, Blickling, Hindolveston, Hemsby, Hindringham, Wiggenhall (St German), Beckham, Martham, Plumstead, Lakenham, Arminghall, Yarmouth, Aldeby, Stoke, Norwich St Stephen, Trowse, Eaton, Scratby, Elmham, Chalk (Kent), Kirkoswald [? Cumbria] and Hopton (Suffolk), 1205.

21. Grant of Thorpe Wood and division of revenue between bishop and monks, 1211.

22. Agreement with priory re churches of Sedgeford, Witton, Blickling, Hindolveston, Hemsby and Hindringham, 1211.

23. Grant to priory of church at Thornham, 1205.

24, 25. Appropriation of church of Beckham to priory, 1205.

26, 27. Appropriation of church of Lakenham to priory, [? 1205]

28. Appropriation of church of Hindringham to priory, [? 1205].

29, 30. Appropriation of church of Hindolveston to priory, [?1205].

31. Grant of church of St Edmund, Hoxne and tithes from assarts of demesne of Homersfield (both in Suffolk), [? 1200-5].

32. Grant of church of Sedgeford, [? 1200-14].

33. Fragment of charter re grants of churches, including Martham, [1200-14].

34, 35. Copies of charters of John de Grey.

THOMAS DE BLUNDEVILLE

36. *Inspeximus* and confirmation of charter of John de Grey, appropriating church of Wiggenhall St German, 1227.

37. Confirmation to hospital of St Paul, Norwich of churches of St Paul, Norwich, St Michael, St Peter, St Andrew and St Margaret, all in Ormesby, tithes of Ormesby, portions of tithes of Blofield, Bacton, Thorpe [unidentified which], Thornage, Langham, Marsham, Blickling, Taverham, Trowse Newton and Filby, 1227.

38. *Inspeximus* and confirmation of charter of Bishop John, appropriating church of St Mary and chapel of St Eustace, Plumstead to priory, 1227.

39. *Inspeximus* and confirmation of charter of Bishop John de Grey, appropriating church of Beckham to priory, 1227.

40. Grant to priory of portions of tithes in Thornage, Langham, Postwick, Wroxham, Swanton [Abbot], Buxton, Hockering, Deopham, Whitlingham, [North] Elmham, Threxton, Scarning, Witchingham, Cockthorpe, Fring, Cressingham and in Homersfield (Suffolk), [? 1227-36].

WILLIAM OF RALEIGH

41. Confirmation of grant of church of Bawburgh to priory, 1241.

42. Confirmation of grant of land in Thornham to priory, 1242.

43. Confirmation of grant of church of Catton to priory, [*c.*1242-43].

WALTER DE SUFFIELD

44. Confirmation of grants of tithes in Thornage, Langham, Postwick, Wroxham, Swanton [Abbot], Buxton, Hockering, Deopham, Shotesham, Intwood, Whitlingham, Cockthorpe, Cressingham, Bircham Newton and in Homersfield (Suffolk), 1245.

45. Appropriation of churches of All Saints, Wicklewood and Hempstead to priory, 1249.

46. Appropriation of church of Worstead, 1256.

47. Grant of land in Thorpe by Norwich to William Ingelond, with consent of priory, [1243-58].

48. Copy of foundation charter of St Giles Hospital, Norwich, [1243-58].

SIMON WALTON

49. Confirmation of grant of watermill and windmill in Thornham to priory, [1258-65].

ROGER SKERNING

50. Confirmation of grant of land to chapel of St Edmund, Hoxne, Suffolk, [1265-78].

51. Grant of rents from messuage in Hoxne, Suffolk, to cell at Hoxne, 1270.

52. *Inspeximus* and confirmation of Bishop Everard's charter founding St Paul's Hospital, 1276.

53. Confirmation of grant of church of Hindolveston to priory, 1277.

54. *Inspeximus* of grant of land in St Peter Parmountergate and St Mary the Less in Norwich to priory, [1269-78].

RALPH WALPOLE

55, 56. Two copies of episcopal decision in dispute between priory and Archdeacon of Suffolk re procurations from churches of Denham and Henley in Suffolk, 1299.

JOHN SALMON

57. Decree re tithes and temporalities of St Stephen's church, Norwich, 1304.

58. Composition between rector of Taverham and priory re tithes from Taverham, 1312.

59-65. Constitution of chapel of St John the Evangelist at the west end of the cathedral as a chantry and appropriation of church of Westhall, Suffolk, for payment of chantry priests, with related documents, 1316-22.

WILLIAM AYERMINE

66. Letter appointing Adam de Ayermine and Richard de Ayermine as collectors of revenue for the Archbishop of Canterbury, 1325.

67. Confirmation of obedience owed to bishop from priests of chantry of Sir Thomas Tilney, 1327.

ANTHONY BEK

68, 69. Grant of payment of 50s. *per annum* from rector of Fring to priory, 1340.

70, 71. Appropriation of church of Ryston and of church of Fordham to the priory, to be used for repairs to the fabric, 1342.

72. Copy of decision in dispute between priory and rector of Gaywood re tithes in Gaywood, [1337-43].

WILLIAM BATEMAN

73. Appropriation of church of Fring to priory, 1352.

THOMAS PERCY

74, 75. Appropriation of church of Sprowston to priory, with agreement for masses to be said for Bishop Thomas and his family, 1361.

76. Bishop's letter re dispute as to priest of St Margaret, Lynn, 1362.

77. Recitation of mandate of Simon, Archbishop of Canterbury re friars in Lynn, 1362.
78. Grant of tithes and fruits of benefice of Tharston and chapel at Stratton, [1356-69].

HENRY DE SPENCER

79. Letter to clergy in Lynn, giving statutes for better regulation of divine office, 1373.
80, 81. Confirmation of appropriation of church of Sprowston, 1385.
82. Mandate to parishioners of Lynn that feast of dedication of church of St Margaret and chapels of St Nicholas and St James is to be celebrated uniformly on 19 October, 1389.
83. Letter to prior of Norwich re custody of muniments, 1395.
84. Fragment of letter to prior of Norwich, reciting order, 1403.

RICHARD NYKKE

85. Decree ordering payment to priory for the chapel in the Bishop's Palace, Norwich, 1508.

JOHN PELHAM

86. Revocation of statute forbidding renewal of leases of property in the Cathedral precincts, 1868.

BISHOPS OF ROCHESTER

87. Bishop Gilbert: grant of Chalk church, [1185-1214].
88, 89. Bishop Hamo de Hethe: appropriation of Chalk to priory, 1326.

DCN 44/ PRE-REFORMATION TITLE DEEDS

These are arranged by place, Norfolk places listed first, followed by out-county places. A smaller number of leases and miscellaneous material stored with the title deeds is included. A few private deeds are included that do not relate to priory property. Some deeds relate to the estate of the bishop rather than the Cathedral. In the following list private deeds are indicated by [P], deeds for bishop's estates by [B]:

Norfolk

1. Aldeby, 1286-1495 and n.d. (19 docs)
2. Alderford, late 13th century-1378. (4 docs)

3. Arminghall, 1313, 1316 and n.d. (3 docs)
4. Attlebridge, late 13th century-1423 and n.d. (23 docs)
5. Barford, 1292, 1451. (2 docs)
6. Barton Bendish [P], 1305. (1 doc)
7. North Barsham, 1338. (2 docs)
8. Bawburgh, late 13th century-1477 and n.d. (34 docs)
9. Bawsey, 13th century. (1 doc)
10. Beetley [P], 1476. (1 doc)
11. Besthorpe, 13th century. (1 doc)
12. Bixley [P], 1316-1331 and n.d. (6 docs)
13. Blickling, 1294-1503. (3 docs)
14. Blofield [B], 1294. (1 doc)
15. Braconash [P], 1316 and n.d. (2 docs)
16. Bracondale, late 13th century-1404. (15 docs)
17. Brundall, 1427. (1 doc)
18. Burgh [not identified which], n.d. (1 doc)
19. South Burlingham [P], 1314. (1 doc)
20. Burnham Thorpe [P], 1307. (1 doc)
21. Buxton, 13th century. (3 docs)
22. Catton, mid 13th century-1331. (10 docs)
23. Clenchwarton, 1350 and n.d. (2 docs)
24. Clippesby [P], 1389. (1 doc)
25. Congham [P], 1323-1348. (7 docs)
26. Coston, Kimberley, Runhall [P], 1368. (1 doc)
27. Cressingham, n.d. (1 doc)
28. South Creake, n.d. (3 docs)
29. Cringleford, mid 13th century and n.d. (16 docs)
30. East Dereham [P], 1312, 1444. (2 docs)
31. Dilham, mid 12th century and n.d. (2 docs)
32. Docking, 1289-1310. (1 doc)
33. Earlham, late 13th century-1405 and n.d. (30 docs)
34. Eaton by Norwich, early 12th century-1473. (9 docs)
35. Eaton by Sedgeford, 1468 and n.d. (3 docs)
36. Elmham, mid 13th century-1380 and n.d. (12 docs)
37. Field Dalling, 1526. (5 docs)
38. Flordon, n.d. (5 docs)
39. Fring, 1351, 1354. (3 docs)
40. Fundenhall [P], 1375. (1 doc)
41. Gateley, mid 13th century-1333. (10 docs)
42. Gaywood, mid 13th Century-1480 and n.d. (19 docs)
43. Glandford [P], n.d. (1 doc)
44. Grimston, n.d. (1 doc)

45.	Hackford, 1340-1410 and n.d.	(4 docs)
46.	Haddiscoe, n.d.	(1 doc)
47.	Hainford, 1343.	(1 doc)
48.	Hapton [P], 1353.	(1 doc)
49.	Hardingham, 1297.	(1 doc)
50.	Harpley, n.d.	(2 docs)
51.	Hautbois, n.d.	(1 doc)
52.	Heacham, 1313 and n.d.	(2 docs)
53.	Heigham, 1312.	(1 doc)
54.	Hellesdon, 1301-1504 and n.d.	(8 docs)
55.	Hemblington, 1424, 1488.	(2 docs)
56.	Hempstead, 1240-1475 and n.d.	(6 docs)
57.	Herringsby, Stokesby, Runham, 1325.	(1 doc)
58.	Hillington [P], 1340-1384.	(5 docs)
59.	Hindolveston, mid 13th century-1492.	(46 docs)
60.	Hindringham, mid 13th century-1483.	(8 docs)
61.	Hoe, n.d.	(2 docs)
62.	Holme next the Sea [P], 1398.	(1 doc)
63.	Houghton, 1301.	(1 doc)
64.	Ingham, 1330.	(1 doc)
65.	Intwood [P], late 13th century.	(2 docs)
66.	Islington, n.d.	(1 doc)
67.	Kerdiston [P], 1299.	(1 doc)
68.	Keswick, late 13th century-1328.	(13 docs)
69.	Ketteringham, n.d.	(1 doc)
70.	Kimberley, 1340-1487 and n.d.	(16 docs)
71.	Kirby [P], n.d.	(1 doc)
72.	Lakenham, 1289-1472 and n.d.	(13 docs)
73.	Langham, 1278-1492.	(7 docs)
	Langley *see* DCN 44/132 below.	
74.	Letheringsett [B], n.d.	(1 doc)
75.	Loddon, n.d.	(4 docs)
76.	Lynn, 13th-15th centuries and n.d.; with leet roll 1311.	(176 docs)
77.	Markshall, n.d.	(4 docs)
78.	Martham, 1287-1462 and n.d.	(9 docs)
79.	Massingham [B], n.d.	(1 doc)
80.	Great Melton, 1311-1376 and n.d.	(12 docs)
81.	Mintlynn, 13th century.	(2 docs)
82.	Morston, late 13th century-1338 and n.d.	(7 docs)
83.	Moulton [P], 1365.	(1 doc)
84.	Norton [P], 1357 and n.d.	(5 docs)
85.	Ormesby, 13th century-1464.	(45 docs)

86.	Outwell, Upwell, 1348-78 and n.d.	(13 docs)
87.	Great Plumstead, 1240-1445.	(15 docs)
87A.	Pockthorpe next Norwich, 13th century-1478.	(15 docs)
88.	Postwick, 1282-1307/27.	(3 docs)
89.	Raveningham, mid 13th century-1414.	(10 docs)
90.	Ringland, 1306.	(1 doc)
91.	Rockland, mid 13th century and n.d.	(14 docs)
92.	Ryston, Fordham 1336.	(1 doc)
93.	Saxlingham, n.d.	(1 doc)
94.	Scottow [P], 1342-47.	(3 docs)
95.	Scratby, mid 13th century-1466 and n.d.	(42 docs)
96.	Sedgeford, early 13th century-1494 and n.d.	(61 docs)
97.	Setchey [P], n.d.	(1 doc)
98.	Shotesham, n.d.	(1 doc)
99.	Smallburgh, n.d.	(1 doc)
100.	Southwood [P], n.d.	(1 doc)
101.	Sparham, 1390.	(1 doc)
102.	Sprowston, 1324-1448.	(5 docs)
103.	Stoke Holy Cross, 1286-1318 and n.d.	(17 docs)
104.	Stratton, n.d.	(2 docs)
105.	Surlingham, mid 13th century and n.d.	(8 docs)
106.	Swainsthorpe [P], 1395.	(1 doc)
107.	Swannington, mid 13th century-1371 and n.d.	(5 docs)
108.	Taverham, late 13th century-1447 and n.d.	(25 docs)
109.	Tharston, n.d.	(2 docs)
110.	Themelthorpe [P], 1300, 1306.	(2 docs)
111.	Thornage [B], 1291.	(2 docs)
112.	Thornham, 1242-1308 and n.d.	(12 docs)
113.	Thorpe next Haddiscoe [P],1307, 1329.	(2 docs)
114.	Thorpe next Norwich, early 13th century-1398.	(41 docs)
115.	Thurlton, 1284-1481 and n.d.	(45 docs)
116.	Thurning, n.d.	(1 doc)
117.	Trowse, mid 13th century-1479 and n.d.	(68 docs)
118.	Welney, n.d.	(1 doc)
119.	Weston, 1394 and n.d.	(3 docs)
120.	Wheatacre, n.d.	(3 docs)
121.	Whitlingham, 1259-1340.	(26 docs)
122.	Wicklewood, mid 13th century-1535.	(13 docs)
123.	Wiggenhall, 1231-1493 and n.d.	(26 docs)
124.	Witchingham, 1220, 1411 and n.d.	(8 docs)
125.	Wolferton [P], 1397, 1403	(2 docs)
126.	Wolterton, n.d.	(3 docs)

127.	Wood Dalling, 13th century and n.d	(5 docs)
128.	Wood Norton, 1284-1490.	(59 docs)
129.	Worstead, Smallburgh, Dilham, 1338.	(1 doc)
130.	Wymondham, 1327-42.	(4 docs)
131.	Yarmouth, early 13th century-1457.	(68 docs)
132.	Langley, n.d.	(2 docs)

Suffolk

133.	Barsham [P], 1286, 1383 and n.d.	(4 docs)
134.	Claydon, 1410-87.	(5 docs)
135.	Helmingham, 1327-49 and n.d.	(11 docs)
136.	Hemmingstone, Witnesham, n.d.	(1 doc)
137.	Henham, n.d.	(1 doc)
138.	Henley, mid 13th century-1324 and n.d.	(29 docs)
139.	Henstead [P], 1377.	(1 doc)
140.	Hopton, mid 13th century-1442 and n.d.	(21 docs)
141.	Hoxne, 1472.	(1 doc)
142.	Ilketshall, n.d.	(1 doc)
143.	Lakenheath [P], 1333.	(1 doc)
144.	Lound, n.d.	(1 doc)
145.	Milden [P], 1379.	(1 doc)
146.	Rushmere, Mutford [P], 1367.	(1 doc)
147.	Sotterley [P], 1377-88.	(6 docs)
148.	Thorpe, n.d.	(1 doc)
149.	Wangford, 1290 and n.d.	(4 docs)
150.	Westhall, 1314-1481	(3 docs)
151.	Witnesham [B], 1286.	(1 doc)

Buckinghamshire

152.	Burnham [P], 1334 and n.d.	(5 docs)

Essex

153.	Lambourne [B], 1259.	(1 doc)
154.	Terling [B], 1227-89 and n.d.	(4 docs)

Kent

155.	Chalk, 1331-61.	(8 docs)

Lincolnshire

156.	Scampton, 1174-1440 and n.d.	(6 docs)

London

157.	Charing [B], 1244x57.	(1 doc)
158.	Westminster [B], 1244x57.	(1 doc)

No place given
159. [P], 1343. (1 doc)

DCN 44a/ TITLE DEEDS TO 19th- and 20th-CENTURY SALES AND PURCHASES

1. Advowson of E. Anstey (Devon), acquired by Chapter, 1900.
2 Land in East Tilney, acquired by Chapter, 1892.
3. Estate in Lakenham, Norwich, sold by Chapter, 1853.
4. Estate in Field Dalling, sold by Chapter, 1900.
5. Estate in Stoke Holy Cross, sold by Chapter, 1853.
6. Marshland in Wheatacre All Saints, sold by Chapter, 1852.
7. Manor of Hindolveston, sold by Chapter, 1853.
8. Manor of Cressingham, sold by Chapter, 1853.
9. Land at Scalby (Yorks), sold by Chapter, 1854.
10. Manor and rectory of Arminghall, sold by Chapter, 1854.
11. Tenements in St George Colegate, Norwich, sold by Chapter, 1853.
12. Land in Thorpe Hamlet, Norwich, sold by Chapter, 1833.
13. Estate in Surlingham, sold by Chapter, 1935.
14. Estate in Sprowston, sold by Chapter, 1857.
15. Advowson of North Lynn, sold by Chapter, 1846.
16. Estate in Martham, sold by Chapter, 1873.
17. Tenements in Bishopgate, Norwich, sold by Chapter, 1857.
18. Tenements in St Paul's, Norwich, sold by Chapter, 1857, 1858.
19. Site of school in St Paul's, Norwich, sold by Chapter, 1864.
20. Estate in St Paul's, Norwich, sold by Chapter, 1853.
21. Estate in St Julian's, Norwich, sold by Chapter, 1867.
22. Estate in St Stephen's, Norwich, sold by Chapter, 1859.

DCN 45/ OLD FOUNDATION: PRIVATE TITLE DEEDS AND LEASES - NORWICH CITY

The deeds are listed by parish in the following order:

1. All Saints Ber Street (Timberhill), 1421. (1 doc)
2. All Saints Fyebridgegate, 13th century-1493. (21 docs)
3. St Andrew, 13th century-1536. (13 docs)
4. St Augustine, 1375. (1 doc)
5. St Benedict, 1407. (1 doc)
   St Botolph *see* St Olave.
6. St Clement Fyebridgegate, 13th century-1369. (3 docs)
7. St Clement (not identified which), 1289. (1 doc)

8. St Cuthbert, 13th century-1331. (33 docs)
9. St Edward, 1289. (1 doc)
10. St Etheldreda, 1285-1322. (3 docs)
11. St George Colegate, 1530. (1 doc)
12. St George Tombland, 13th century-1529. (37 docs)
13. St George (not identified which), 13th century. (3 docs)
14. St Giles, 13th century. (2 docs)
15. St Gregory, 13th century-1535. (18 docs)
16. St James, 13th century-1505. (10 docs)
17. St John Maddermarket, 13th century-1499. (14 docs)
18. St John De Ber Street (Timberhill), 13th century-1379. (10 docs)
19. St John Sepulchre, 1486, 1536. (3 docs)
20. St Lawrence, 1306, 1308. (2 docs)
21. St Margaret Fyebridgegate, 13th century. (1 doc)
22. St Martin Bailey, 1491. (1 doc)
23. St Martin at Palace, 1282. (1 doc)
24. St Martin Coslany, 13th century, 1426. (2 docs)
25. St Mary Coslany, 13th century-1412. (5 docs)
26. St Mary in the Marsh, 13th century-1535. (9 docs)
    St Mary in Combusto *see* St Saviour.
27. St Mary Parva, 1269-1392. (9 docs)
28. St Michael at Plea, 1283-1525. (19 docs)
    St Michael at Thorn *see* St Vedast.
29. St Michael Conesford, 1308. (1 doc)
30. St Olave, *c.*1256-1492. Includes 2 references to St Botolph. (9 docs)
31. St Paul, 13th century-1534. (34 docs)
32. St Peter Hungate, 1277-1441. (20 docs)
33. St Peter Mancroft, 13th century-1401. (66 docs)
34. St Peter Parmountergate, 13th century-1537. (25 docs)
35. St Saviour, 13th century. Includes 1 reference to St Mary in Combusto. (4 docs)
36. SS Simon and Jude, 1403. (1 doc)
37. St Stephen, 1256-1537. (23 docs)
38. St Vedast, *c.*1200-1466. Includes 1 reference to St Michael at Thorn. (14 docs)
39. Deeds covering a large number of parishes, 13th century-1316. (8 docs)
40. Deeds where no parish is named, 13th century-1512. (60 docs)

DCN 46/ TITLE DEEDS AND OTHER DOCUMENTS RELATING TO EAST ANGLIAN RELIGIOUS HOUSES

BURY ST EDMUNDS

1-24. Title deeds to property at Chelsworth (Suffolk), 1312-77.

25. Bailiff's account roll Chelsworth, 1391.

26. Bailiff's account roll Chelsworth, 1427-8.

CRABHOUSE NUNNERY

27. Transcript of appropriation of medietaty of church of St Peter, Wiggenhall, to Crabhouse, 1313.

ST FELIX WALTON, ESSEX

28-32. Title deeds to property at Ramsey (Essex), 1250, 1295 and n.d.

33-37. Title deeds to land at Aspall, Felixstowe and Trimley (Suffolk), 14th century.

IPSWICH HOLY TRINITY

38. Visitation of priory, 1336.

WALSINGHAM

39. Notification by Margaret de Cressy to Reinald de Ely that she has granted his homage and service to Walsingham, n.d.

HORSHAM ST FAITH

40. Grant of land in Horsham to the priory there, 1240.

IXWORTH, SUFFOLK

41, 42. Grants to Ixworth of property in Suffolk, 1296, 1309.

ESTATE LEASES

DCN 47/ LEDGER BOOKS

Registers containing copies of leases granted. The early volumes include copies of correspondence and other documents.

1.	1538-*c.*1562.
2.	*c.*1559-65.
3.	1565-1631.
4.	1625-49, 1660-68.
5.	1668-87.
6.	1687-98.
7.	1698-1715.
8.	1715-27.
9.	1727-36.
10.	1737-49.
11.	1749-61.
12.	1761-71.
13.	1771-80.
14.	1780-9.
15.	1789-98.
16.	1798-1809.
17.	1810-20.
18.	1820-5.
19.	1825-35.
20.	1835-43.
21.	1843-50.
22.	1850-6.
23.	1856-63.
24.	1863-82.
25.	1883-1932.

DCN 47A LEASES BY DEAN GARDINER

Copies of two leases by Dean Gardiner to Elizabeth I, leasing cathedral estates and manors to her for term of one hundred years, 1 February 1579, 25 August 1581.

DCN 48 CHAPTER LEASES: CITY OF NORWICH

Original leases for estates in parishes of All Saints, St Andrew, St George

Colegate (including site of former church of St Olave), St George Timberhill (including former parish of St Mary the Less), St Giles, St Gregory, St James Pockthorpe (with map of osier ground, 1714, papers and plans re cavalry barracks, 19th century), St John Maddermarket (including site of former church of St Crowche), St John Timberhill, St Julian, St Martin at Oak, St Martin at Palace, St Mary in the Marsh (including lease of meadow to Sir Thomas Browne with his signature), St Michael at Plea, St Michael at Thorn (including former parish of St Martin in the Bailey), St Paul (including former parish of All Saints Fyebridgegate), St Peter Hungate, St Peter Mancroft, St Peter Parmountergate (including former parish of St Vedast), St Saviour and St Stephen.

DCN 49/ CHAPTER LEASES: NORFOLK, SUFFOLK AND YORKSHIRE

Original leases of Chapter estates. A few private title deeds have become intermixed with these leases and are noted below.

Norfolk

1.	Aldeby	Estate leases, 1535, 1839, 1853.	(3 docs)
2.	Arminghall	Estate leases, 1534, 1576-1881.	(37 docs)
3.	Attlebridge	Estate leases, 1565-1742.	(13 docs)
4.	Barford	Estate leases, 1504, 1580-1854.	(12 docs)
5.	Bawburgh	Estate leases, 1529, 1554-1855.	(9 docs)
6.	Beckham, West		
		Estate leases, 1510, 1539-1863.	(11 docs)
7.	Beetley	Estate leases, 1545.	(1 doc)
8.	Blofield	No estate leases.	
		Private title deeds, 1800-28.	(3 docs)
9.	Buxton	Estate leases, 1616-83.	(6 docs)
10.	Catton	Estate leases, 1538-1865.	(15 docs)
	Colkirk *see* Gateley.		
11.	Cressingham, Great		
		Estate leases, 1675, 1683.	(3 docs)
12.	Dilham, Horning	No estate leases.	
		Leases issued by the Bishop of Ely, 1623-1868.	(19 docs)
13.	Dillington	Estate leases, 1849, 1863.	(2 docs)
14.	Eaton	Estate leases, 1528-1871, with estate papers.	(*c*.40 docs)
15.	Ellingham, Great		
		No estate leases. Private title deeds, 1783-1834.	(13 docs)
16.	Elmham, North		
		Estate leases, 1469, 1496, 1550-1692.	(11 docs)
17.	Field Dalling	Estate leases, 1526, 19th century.	(5 docs)
	Foldholme and Skeetholme Marshes *see* Yarmouth.		
18.	Fordham	Estate leases, 1664, 1680.	(2 docs)
	Fordham *see also* Ryston.		

19.	Fring	Estate leases, 1678-1862, with papers re dispute over parsonage, water colour paintings of parsonage, plan of Fring parish, all early 19th century.	(*c*. 50 docs)
20.	Gateley, Colkirk	Estate leases, 1631-1679.	(9 docs)
21.	Gaywood	Estate leases, 1552-1863.	(11 docs)
22.	Gnatingdon	Estate lease, 1501. Later leases for this estate are included under Sedgeford.	(1 doc)
23.	Halvergate	No estate leases. Leases issued by the Bishop of Ely, 1633-1851.	(40 docs)
24.	Heigham	No estate leases. Order of exchange of lands between Bishop of Norwich and Dean and Chapter, 1859, with related papers.	(2 docs)
25.	Hemblington	Estate leases, 1519, 1535, 1580-1682.	(14 docs)
26.	Hempnall	No estate leases. Private leases, 1829, 1837.	(2 docs)
27.	Hempstead	Estate leases, 1544-1851.	(11 docs)
28.	Hemsby, Martham	Copy of conveyance by Court of Augmentation of property lately belonging to Norwich Cathedral, 1562.	(1 doc)
29.	Hevingham, Marsham	Lease of portion of tithes, 1568-1854.	(11 docs)
30.	Hindolveston	Estate leases, 1491, 1537, 1574-1801.	(14 docs)
31.	Hindringham	Estate leases, 1505, 1563-1857.	(10 docs)
32.	Hoe	Estate leases, 1562-1867.	(14 docs)
33.	Horning	No estate leases. Leases by Bishop of Norwich, 1545, 1640.	(2 docs)
34.	Ingham	No estate leases. Leases by Bishop of Norwich, 1689-1850.	(23 docs)
35.	Islington	No estate leases. Private title deeds, 1626, 1628.	(2 docs)
36.	Langham	No estate leases. Conveyance to Bishop of Norwich, 1731.	(7 docs)
37.	Lakenham	Estate leases, 1496, 1502, 1545-1834.	(20 docs)
38.	Lynn	Estate leases, 1570-1848.	(13 docs)
	Marsham *see* Hevingham.		
39.	Martham	Estate leases, 1539, 1551-1673.	(11 docs)
	Martham *see also* Hemsby.		
40.	Moulton, Aslacton	No estate leases. Private lease, 1843.	(1 doc)

41. Ormesby Estate leases with related papers, 1578-1856. (15 docs)

42. Plumstead, Great
Estate leases, 1535-1824. (7 docs)

43. Plumstead, Little
No estate leases. Private leases, 1825-27. (3 docs)

44. Plumstead, Great and Little
Estate leases, 1858, 1893. (2 docs)

45. Pulham St Mary Magdalen
No estate leases. Private title deeds, 17th-18th centuries. (19 docs)

Raveningham *see* Thurlton

46. Repps No estate leases. Private title deeds, 17th-18th centuries. (15 docs)

47. Riston and Roxham
Estate leases, 1564-1864. (6 docs)

48. Ruston, East
No estate leases. Lease by Bishop of Norwich, 1846. (1 doc)

49. Sedgeford Estate leases and related papers, 1584-1861.(9 docs)

50. Sprowston Estate leases, 1509-1863. (15 docs)

51. Stoke Holy Cross
Estate leases, 1507, 1587-1800. (10 docs)

52. Strumpshaw
No estate leases. Private title deeds, 1827-41.(4 docs)

53. Surlingham Estate leases, 1646-1730. (4 docs)

54. Taverham Estate leases, 1542-1677. (4 docs)

55. Tharston Estate leases, 1606, with leases by Bishop of Ely, 1827-49. (33 docs)

56. Thorpe next Norwich
Estate leases, 1488, 1519, 1541-1866. (40 docs)

57. Thurlton and Raveningham
Estate lease, 1493. (1 doc)

58. Trowse Estate leases, 1547-1861. (30 docs)

59. Upwell Estate leases, 1627-1865 ,with private title deeds, 1746-71. (31 docs)

60. Wheatacre Estate leases, 1543-1661. (4 docs)

61. Whitwell Estate leases, 1544-1862. (11 docs)

62. Wiggenhall Estate leases, 1485, 1496, 1563-1862. (11 docs)

63. Wighton Estate leases, 1492, 1518, 1562-1862. (11 docs)

64.	Witchingham, Great	No estate leases. Private title deeds, *c.*1843.	(1 bundle)
65.	Worstead	Estate leases, 1488, 1556-1861.	(11 docs)
66.	Yarmouth	Estate leases for Yarmouth Rectory, 1781-1862.	(2 docs)
		Estate leases for Foldholme and Skeetholme marshes, 1483, 1553-1860.	(15 docs)
67.	Unidentified	Private lease, 1678.	(1 doc)

Suffolk

68.	Bungay	No estate leases. Miscellaneous leases, 1817.	(2 docs)
69.	Elmham, South	Estate leases, 1519, 1524, 1552, 1637.	(5 docs)
70.	Henley	Estate leases, 1567-1862.	(6 docs)
71.	Hopton	Estate leases, 1501, 1528, 1602-1857.	(20 docs)
72.	Hoxne	No estate leases. Episcopal title deed, 1724.	(1 doc)
73.	Ilketshall St Margaret	No estate leases. Miscellaneous lease, 1849.	(1 doc)
74.	Spexhall	No estate leases. Miscellaneous lease, 1831.	(1 doc)
75.	Westhall	Estate leases, 1595-1859.	(13 docs)

Yorkshire

76.	Scalby	Estate leases, 1575-1776.	(35 docs)

DCN 50/ TITHE RENT CHARGE PAPERS

Deeds and documents transferred to the Dean and Chapter when they were granted tithe rent charges in exchange for estates. 1-5 were granted in exchange for the estate at Middleton in 1887. 6-16 were granted in exchange for estates at Plumstead, Tilney St Lawrence, Islington, Foldholme and Skeetholme Marshes, Wingfield (Suffolk), Frostenden (Suffolk), Woodham Walter (Essex) in 1894. The tithe rent charge at Wingfield (DCN 50/18) was in fact held by the Dean and Chapter but when the estates at Wingfield were surrendered in 1894 it was at that stage proposed that the rent charge should be given up too. This was not carried out, but the documents passed through the hands of the Ecclesiastical Commissioners and have been numbered by them.

1.	Crimplesham, 1814-90.	(4 docs)
2.	Great Plumstead, Witton, Brundall, *c.*1884.	(3 docs)

3.	Ridlington, Walcott, *c.*1851.	(7 docs)
4.	Ringland, 1692-1854.	(23 docs)
5.	Hopton (Suffolk), *c.*1857.	(4 docs)
6.	Bawburgh, 1799-1855.	(7 docs)
7.	West Bradenham, 1762-1856.	(24 docs)
8.	Buxton, 1811-68.	(7 docs)
9.	Hindringham, 1800-73.	(7 docs)
10.	Kenninghall, 1804-*c.*1845.	(3 docs)
11.	Loddon, 1857.	(1 doc)
12.	Narford, 1634-1852.	(26 docs)
13.	Sedgeford, 1800-74.	(4 docs)
14.	Whitwell, 1800-62.	(8 docs)
15.	Wighton, 1789-1862.	(8 docs)
16.	Worstead, *c.*1868.	(3 docs)
17.	Schedule of deeds, etc. now DCN 50/6-16 above.	
18.	Wingfield (Suffolk), *c.*1895.	(20 docs)

RENTALS AND SURVEYS

DCN 51/ RENTALS, SURVEYS AND VALUATIONS

Rentals, surveys and valuations not in volume form are listed as DCN 51, those in volume form as DCN 52. Some rentals and surveys are bound into the Libri Miscellaneorum: *see* DCN 29 list.

1-3.	Aldeby, Prior's Manor: rentals, 1683-1799.
4.	Amners under the Oak Manor: rental, 1799.
5.	Arminghall: extent, with summary of charters re common pasture and transcript of agreement between almoner of Holy Trinity and rector of Caistor St Edmund 14th century.
6.	Arminghall Manor: rental, 1799.
7.	Attlebridge: terrier, *c.*1770.
8.	Attlebridge Rectory Estate: terrier, 1770.
9.	Bawburgh Estate: terrier, 1512.
10.	Bawburgh Rectory Estate: copy of Parliamentary Survey, 1650.
11.	Barton Turf, Crostwight, East Ruston: custumal, [14th century].
12.	Brampton: answers to queries re state of house and land, 1719.
13.	Bracondale: list of tithes paid, [14th century].
14.	Catton Manor: copy of Parliamentary Survey, 1649.
15.	Catton Manor: rental, 1799.
16.	Catton, Sprowston: lands owing tithes to almoner, [14th century].
17.	Chelsworth, Suffolk: rental, [14th century].
18.	Great Cressingham Manor: rental, 1799.
19.	Cringleford: terrier, [18th century].
20.	Dilham: list of tenants, with transcript of charters, [early 14th century].
21-25.	Eaton Manor: rentals and related papers, 16th-18th centuries.
26-33.	North Elmham Chapter Estate: rentals and related papers, 1552-1799.
34-36.	Field Dalling, Wolterton and Gibbs Manor: terriers and rentals, 1640-1799.
37.	Hellesdon, Catton: terrier of lands leased to Mary Green, [17th century].
38.	Hellesdon, Tolthorpe: extent, [15th century].
39.	Hempstead, Baconsthorpe: rental, [18th century].
40.	Henley Manor, Suffolk: rental, [18th century].
41.	Hindolveston Manor: custumal, [13th century].
42-47.	Hindolveston Manor: terriers, rentals, 1683-1812.
48.	Hindringham Manor: rental, 1799.
49, 50.	Hoe, Pakenham and Giles Manor: terriers, 17th century and 1772.
51.	Hopton Manor, Suffolk: rental, [14th century].

52-56. Hopton Manor, Suffolk: rentals, terriers, 1533-1808.
57. Kimberley, Prior's Manor: rental 1505, with undated rentals and with court book, 1434/5-1477/8.
58. Kimberley: copy of Parliamentary Survey, 1649.
59. Lakenham, Trowse: rental, [14th century].
60. Langham: terrier of land owing tithes to Holy Trinity, [*c.*1460].
61. Marsham, Hevingham: terrier of land owing tithes to Holy Trinity, [18th century].
62. Marsham: rental, 1497.
63-65. Martham: terriers, valuations, 1752-1858.
66-68. Morston: rentals, 1542, 1597, 1799.
69. Newton in Trowse: copy of Parliamentary Survey, 1649.
70. Newton in Trowse: terrier, 1728.
71. Newton in Trowse: rental, 1799.
72. Norton, Guist: extent, 1397-8.
73. Norton, Guist: rental, [15th century].
74. Norton, Guist, Hindolveston: rental, 1537-38.
Norwich, *see* DCN 51/122-151.
75. Ormesby, Scratby: terrier, 1705.
76. Outwell, Upwell: terrier, 1739.
77. Outwell, Upwell, Emneth: rental, 1396/7.
78. Great Plumstead: note re cellarer's land, [15th century].
79. Great Plumstead: copy of Parliamentary Survey of 1650.
80. Great Plumstead: glebe terrier, 1734.
81. Postwick, Plumstead: rental, 1477-8.
82. Raveningham: terrier of lands owing tithes to priory, [14th century].
83. Ryston, Roxham: copy of Parliamentary Survey of 1649.
84, 85. Sedgeford Manor: rentals, [13th century].
86-88. Sedgeford: surveys of fee held of manor of Brandeston, with related memoranda, 1311, 1338.
89. Sedgeford: rental, 1422-3.
90. Sedgeford, Heacham: survey, [15th century].
91. Sedgeford: copy of Parliamentary Survey of 1649.
92. Sedgeford: notes re lands disputed between Chapter and Thomas Le Strange, [18th century].
93. Sedgeford, Fring, Docking: list of holdings with transcript of charters, [14th century].
94. Sedgeford: extent, [14th century].
95. Sedgeford: rental, 1799.
96. Stoke Holy Cross: glebe terrier, 1775.
97. Swardeston, Mulbarton: rental, 1478.

98-101. Taverham Manor: rentals, surveys, [15th century].
102. Taverham, Keswick, Swardeston, Weston Longville: rental of pitancer's estates, 1478.
103-105. Taverham: terriers and related documents, [16th century].
106. Thornham Manor: survey, [15th century].
107. Thornham: terrier, 1515.
108. Thornham: rentals, 1642, 1649.
109. Thornham: extent, [14th century].
110. Thornham: rental, 1799.
111, 112. Thorpe by Norwich: measurements of woodland, [13th century].
113. Westhall, Suffolk: glebe terrier, 1777.
114. Wicklewood, Deopham: extent, 1487.
115. Wood Norton: rental, [16th century].
116. Worstead: terrier, 1409.
117. Worstead Manor: rental, 1799.
118. Worstead, Dilham, Smallburgh: rental, 1553-57.
119. Worstead, North Elmham: rental, 1688.
120. Worstead, Ryston, Roxham: notes re rents, [18th century].
121. Worstead: glebe terrier, 1784.
122-128. Norwich City: rentals, 14th-15th centuries.
129-135. Norwich City: accounts of rent collectors, 1552-74.
136-151. Norwich City: rentals and related papers, 16th-19th centuries.
152. Valuation of chapter property, 16th century.
153-160. Unidentified and incomplete rentals, 16th-17th century.

DCN 52/ RENTALS, SURVEYS AND VALUATIONS IN VOLUME FORM

1. Parliamentary Survey: Amners under the Oak, Norwich; Amners St Andrew, Worstead; Pockthorpe and Normans manor, Norwich; Lakenham rectory; Worstead rectory; Catton manor and rectory; Trowse mills and land; land in Thorpe St Andrew; Fring rectory and manor; Trowse rectory; Whitwell rectory; Hindringham manor and rectory; Sedgeford manor (East Hall and West Hall) and rectory; Yarmouth priory; Aldeby manor and rectory; Martham rectory; Foldholme and Skeetholme marshes; Trowse Newton manor; land in Gateley and Colkirk; Bawburgh rectory; Riston and Roxham rectory; Great Plumstead rectory; Kimberley manor; Hopton rectory and manor (Suffolk); Scalby rectory, (Yorks), *c.*1649.

2. Volume entitled 'Surveys and Valuations', relating to: Aldeby, Arminghall, Almary Marsh (in Wheatacre), Attlebridge,

Barford, Bawburgh, West Beckham, Carrow Meadow (in Norwich), Catton, Cressingham, Eaton, North Elmham, Fordham, Foldholme and Skeetholme marshes, Fring, Gateley and Colkirk, Gaywood, Hemblington, Hempstead, Hindolveston, Hindringham, Kimberley, Lakenham, Lynn, Martham, Trowse Newton, Norwich, Ormesby and Scratby, Outwell with Upwell and Welney, Pakenham and Giles in Hoe, Plumstead, Pockthorpe (outside Norwich), Riston and Roxham, Sedgeford, Sprowston, Stoke Holy Cross, Surlingham, Taverham, Thorpe by Norwich, Wheatacre, Whitwell, Wiggenhall St Germans, Wighton, Wolterton and Gibbs in Field Dalling, Worstead, Yarmouth: Henley, Hopton, Oulton and Westhall (all Suffolk): Scalby (Yorks), 1683-1816.

3. Volume entitled 'Copies of Surveys', containing 18th-century copies of the Parliamentary Survey of 1649, Hemblington terrier of 1717, field book for Sedgeford, n.d.; inventories of cathedral goods, 1710, 1724, 1725; inventories of singing books, 1715, 1724.

4. Volume containing surveys of Attlebridge, Taverham, Fordham, Kimberley, Bawburgh, Great Cressingham, 1483-1572.

5. Volume containing surveys of Norton, Guist, 1488-89. With manor court accounts for Norton, Guist, 1488-1516 and for Morston, *c.*1509-97.

6, 7. Surveys of North Elmham, 16th century.

8. Survey of Sedgeford, 1454-55.

9. Sedgeford field book, 1736.

10. Cressingham field book, 1646-59.

11-13. Three copies of Eaton field book, 17th century.

14-21. Surveys of Catton, 1470-1606.

22. Volume of valuations covering Aldeby, Arminghall, Barford, Bawburgh, West Beckham, Great Cressingham, Eaton, Fordham, Fring, Foldholme and Skeetholme marshes, Field Dalling, Gaywood, Hempstead, Hindringham, Hoe, Lakenham, Lynn, Martham, estates in Norwich (not including the precinct), Outwell

with Upwell and Welney, Ormesby with Scratby, Great and Little Plumstead, Riston and Roxham, Sedgeford, Sprowston, Stoke Holy Cross, Surlingham, Trowse, Almary marshes in Wheatacre, Wiggenhall St. German, Whitwell, Wighton, Worstead; also Henley, Hopton, Oulton marsh and Westhall in Suffolk, 1804-26.

23. Hindringham field book, 15th century.

24. Surveys of chapter estates in Norwich, with plans, 1811-60.

ESTATE PAPERS

DCN 53-58

Papers arranged by subject.

53. Inclosure Papers, 18th-19th centuries.

54. Papers re Nar Valley drainage, 1857-85.

55. Papers re Lynn and Fakenham Railway, 1881-82.

56. Dilapidations papers, houses in the Close, 1873-1941.

Papers arranged by place.

57. The Close, 19th-20th centuries.

58. Other estates in Norwich, 18th-20th centuries.

DCN 59/

County and out-county estates.

Summary list (detailed lists are available in the Record Office).

1.	Acle, 1891.	(2 docs)
2.	Aldeby, 1725-1857.	(8 docs)
3.	Alderford, 1799.	(1 doc)
4.	Arminghall, 17th century, 1781.	(2 docs)
5.	Attlebridge, 18th century.	(3 docs)
6.	Barford, 1727, 1799.	(2 docs)
7.	Blofield, 1860.	(1 file)
8.	Buxton, 1860.	(1 file)
9.	Catton, 1575-1795.	(18 docs)
10.	Great Cressingham, including Cressingham Magna cum Collins manor suit roll, 1665, abstract of court roll, 1667. 1635-19th-century.	(14 docs)
11.	Earlham, building account for house of Sir John Fastolf at Earlham (in English), 15th century.	(1 doc)

12. Eaton, papers and correspondence re Eaton estate, including 17th- and 18th- century papers re dispute as to ownership of land at Eaton, churchwardens' rates for 9 years between 1661 and 1681; poor rate and other rate assessments, 17th century; bundle of late 19th-century estate correspondence: farming account book of Mr Aldrich of Eaton, 1664-67. (*c*.500 docs)
13. North Elmham, *c*.1740. (8 docs)
14. Field Dalling, 18th century. (7 docs)
15. Foldholme and Skeetholme Marshes, including bundle of estate correspondence and sale particulars, drainage papers, late 19th century.
16. Fordham, *c*.1757. (9 docs)
17. Frettenham, 1693. (1 doc)
18. Gateley and Colkirk, 18th century. (1 doc)
19. Great Hautbois, Coltishall, bundle of title deeds (non cathedral), 1681-1781. (38 docs)
20. Hemblington, 1716-1805. (4 docs)
21. Hindolveston, notes re timber, 1731. (6 docs)
22. Hindringham, correspondence, etc., 18th century. (40 docs)
23. Lakenham, papers re Lakenham rectory, *c*.1770-1825. (22 docs)
24. Ludham, letter re episcopal estates, 1853. (1 doc)
25. Lynn, account for repairs at church, 1698: papers re repairs to church, 18th century. (11 docs)
26. Martham,16th century. (2 docs)
27. Middleton, estate correspondence, with related papers,19th century. (14 bundles, 4 docs)
28. Moulton All Saints, 1663. (3 docs)
29. Plumstead, correspondence, papers, sale particulars, 1636-1891 (mainly 19th century). (12 docs)
30. Sedgeford, papers, correspondence, notes, sale particulars, 18th-19th centuries including correspondence re work at church and parsonage (with plans of parsonage) 1840-42. (6 bundles)
31. Sprowston, 1713, 1804. (3 docs)
32. Starston, 1891. (2 docs)
33. Stoke Holy Cross, land tax, 1719. (1 doc)
34. Surlingham, correspondence, 1884, 1885. (2 docs)
35. Taverham,17th-18th centuries. (8 docs)
36. Thorpe, estate papers and correspondence papers re development of estates at Thorpe Hamlet for housing, late 19th century. (12 bundles)
37. Tilney, 1855-92, with poster for Garden Society annual show. (3 bundles)
38. Trowse, agreement re enclosure, 1567; 18th- and 19th-century papers, including copy of Parliamentary survey. (4 docs)
39. Upwell, 18th-19th centuries. (2 docs)

40. Wacton, vestry minutes and poor rate accounts, 1769-98. (1 vol)

41. Wiggenhall St German, notes re estate and church and re Fordham church, with verse monumental inscriptions, 1734. (1 doc)

42. Witchingham, 1860. (1 doc)

43. Worstead, agreement re church, 1595: specifications for parsonage house, 1841. (For plan of the house see DCN 127/60). (8 docs)

44. Yarmouth, estate papers, etc., 1715-1869, including form of consecrating St George's Chapel, 1715. (14 docs)

Suffolk

45. Frostenden, estate correspondence with two maps of estate, 1876-94. (11 bundles)

46. Henley, 17th-18th centuries. (3 docs)

47. Hopton, 17th-18th centuries. (2 docs)

47A. Oulton Marsh, 1700. (2 docs)

48. Westhall, 18th-19th centuries, including plans of vicarage house, 1861. (4 docs)

49. Wingfield, estate correspondence, sale particulars, late 19th century. (6 bundles)

Essex

50. Woodham Walter, sale particular, 1847, estate bills and correspondence, late 19th-century, plans, etc., for 2 estate cottages, 1875. (*c.*500 docs)

Kent

51. Chalk, letters, 1701, 1705. (3 docs)

Yorkshire

52. Scalby, estate papers, 17th-20th centuries, including plan for new vicarage, 1778. (*c.*75 docs)

Unidentified

53. Estate papers, no obvious identification, 18th-19th centuries. (*c.* 20 papers)

MANORIAL RECORDS

MANOR COURT RECORDS AND BAILIFF'S ACCOUNTS

The main series of manor court records and bailiff's accounts are for the 16 'prior's manors' listed in the Introduction. There are also substantial series for the obedientaries' manors of Aldeby, Amners under the Oak [primarily the precinct area], Great Cressingham and Henley in Suffolk. There are small series of rolls for estates or manors at Arminghall, Attlebridge, Bawburgh, Lakenham, Norwich Norman's Hospital manor, Pockthorpe and Costessey. For some years there are grouped bailiff's accounts or manor court rolls where records from several estates are collected together in one roll or volume. Manor court records for Felthorpe with Tolthorpe have long been stored with these records, but are presumably strays from the diocesan archives, as this manor was an episcopal manor from the mid seventeenth century, having previously been in private hands. A manor court book for Bromholme priory is also presumably a stray. Later manor court records for cathedral manors are among the Church Commissioners' Norwich Chapter Estates records in the Norfolk Record Office.

DCN 60/ MANOR COURT ROLLS AND BAILIFF'S ACCOUNT ROLLS

1.	Aldeby: manor court rolls, 1273-1681.	(11 rolls)
2.	Aldeby: bailiff's account roll, 1312.	(1 roll)
3.	Amners under the Oak (Norwich): manor court rolls, 1344-1573.	(10 rolls, 1 volume)
4.	Catton: bailiff's account rolls, 1265-1623.	(111 rolls)
5.	Catton: manor court rolls and books, 1327-1645.	(9 rolls, 5 volumes)
6.	Great Cressingham: manor court rolls, 1561-1639.	(1 roll, 1 volume)
7.	Denham (Suffolk): bailiff's account rolls, 1273-1318.	(7 rolls)
8.	Eaton: bailiff's account rolls, 1263-1523.	(29 rolls)
9.	Eaton: manor court rolls, 1288-1622	(17 rolls)
10.	North Elmham: bailiff's account rolls, 1255-1523.	(46 rolls)
11.	North Elmham: manor court rolls, 1290-1638.	(24 rolls)
12.	Felthorpe with Tolthorpe [Bishop's Manor]: manor court rolls, 1418-1685.	(13 rolls, 1 volume)
13.	Gateley: bailiff's account rolls, 1263-1411.	(31 rolls)
14.	Gnatingdon: bailiff's account rolls, 1255-1350.	(25 rolls)
15.	Hemsby: bailiff's account rolls, 1265-1335.	(16 rolls)
16.	Henley (Suffolk): bailiff's account rolls, 1282-?1340.	(6 rolls)
17.	Henley (Suffolk): manor court rolls, 1583-1640.	(2 rolls)

18.	Hindolveston: bailiff's account rolls, 1255-1522.	(76 rolls)
19.	Hindolveston: manor court rolls, 1257-1633.	(62 rolls)
20.	Hindringham: bailiff's account rolls, 1255-1526.	(45 rolls)
21.	Hindringham: manor court rolls 1263-1721	(20 rolls)
22.	Martham: manor court rolls, 1288-1552.	(45 rolls)
23.	Martham: bailiff's account rolls, 1261-1523.	(30 rolls)
24.	Melton: manor court rolls, 1286-1392.	(7 rolls)
25.	Melton: bailiff's account rolls, 1332-1469.	(5 rolls)
26.	Monks Grange (outside Norwich): bailiff's account rolls, 1255-1409.	(26 rolls)
27.	Newton: manor court rolls, 1268-1639.	(26 rolls)
28.	Newton: bailiff's account rolls, 1273-1480.	(11 rolls)
29.	Plumstead: bailiff's account rolls, ?1263-1420.	(45 rolls)
30.	Scratby: bailiff's account rolls, 1295-1363.	(12 rolls)
31.	Scratby: manor court rolls, 1350-1444.	(2 rolls)
32.	Sedgeford: manor court rolls, 1256-1692.	(38 rolls, 3 volumes)
33.	Sedgeford: bailiff's account rolls, 1255-1513,	(35 rolls)
34.	Taverham: manor court rolls, 1299-1649.	(14 rolls)
35.	Taverham: bailiff's account rolls, 1255-1565.	(35 rolls)
36.	Thornham: manor court rolls, 1267-1633.	(17 rolls)
37.	Thornham: bailiff's account rolls, 1264-1352.	(21 rolls)
	For Trowse *see* Newton.	
38.	Worstead: manor court rolls and books, 1307-1638.	(15 rolls, 5 volumes)
39.	Worstead: bailiff's account rolls, 1269-1366.	(26 rolls)

DCN 61/ MANOR COURT ROLLS AND BAILIFF'S ACCOUNTS NOT BOXED BY MANOR

ARMINGHALL, LAKENHAM

1-5.	Manor court rolls, 1273-1597, many missing years.	(5 rolls)
6-9.	Bailiff's accounts for Arminghall, 1348-1523.	(4 rolls)
10-12.	Bailiff's accounts for Lakenham, 1297-1464.	(3 rolls)
13.	Memorandum of leases, sales, etc., 1251-67.	(1 doc)

NORWICH LE GANNOCK

14.	Servant's accounts, 1321.	(1 roll)

ATTLEBRIDGE

15-17.	Bailiff's accounts, 1309, 1316 and n.d.	(3 rolls)

BAWBURGH

18-24.	Bailiff's accounts, 1297-1339.	(7 rolls)

BECKHAM, CREAKE, BARFORD, WITCHINGHAM

25.	Bailiff's account, 14th century.	(1 roll)

CATTON, MONKS' GRANGE, CHEDGRAVE, TROWSE

26.	Bailiff's account, 14th century.	(1 roll)

FIELD DALLING: MANOR OF WOLTERTON AND GIBBS

27, 28.	Court rolls, 1519-1697, with many gaps.	(2 rolls)

FORDHAM

29.	Custodian's account, 1345.	(1 roll)

FRING

30.	Bailiff's account, 1498-99.	(1 roll)

HARDINGHAM

31.	Tithe account, 1329.	(1 roll)

HEMSBY

32.	Extract from court roll, 1431.	(1 roll)

HEYTHE IN PLUMSTEAD

33, 34.	Custodian's accounts, 1346, 1366.	(2 rolls)

MORSTON

35-37.	Court rolls, 1417-1597, many gaps.	(3 rolls)

NORWICH, NORMAN'S HOSPITAL

38.	Court book, 1532-1630.	(1 vol)

ORMESBY

39-41.	Bailiff's accounts, 1296-1339.	(3 rolls)

POSTWICK

42, 43.	Bailiff's accounts, 1432-33, 1441-42.	(2 rolls)

TAVERHAM

44.	Farmer's account, 1516-17.	(1 roll)

WICKLEWOOD

45.	Servant's account, 1339.	(1 roll)

WIGGENHALL

46.	Bailiff's account, 1302.	(1 roll)

WITTON

47.	Tithe account, 1274.	(1 roll)
48.	Bailiff's account, 1273.	(1 roll)

SUFFOLK, HOPTON

49, 50.	Court rolls, 1436-1549, many gaps.	(2 rolls)

KENT, CHALK

51.	Tithe account, 1337.	(1 roll)
52.	Servant's account, 1342.	(1 roll)

UNIDENTIFIED

53-55.	Unidentified fragments.	(3 docs)

NON-CATHEDRAL

STOKE (probably STOKE BY NAYLAND, SUFFOLK)

56.	Bailiff's account, 1407-8.	(1 roll)
57.	Manor court roll: four courts in unidentified year.	(1 roll)

NEWTON, KENT

58.	Manor court roll, 1484-85.	(1 roll)

DCN 62/ GROUPED MANOR ACCOUNTS

1. Martham, Plumstead, Monks' Grange, Thornham, Gateley, Taverham, Elmham, Gnatingdon, Catton and one unidentified, 1 William de Castleton [1326-27].

2. Martham, Plumstead, Heythe, Monks' Grange, Catton, Eaton, Taverham, Gateley, Elmham, Hindolveston, Gnatingdon, Sedgeford. With Sedgeford and Elmham tithes, 8 William de Castleton [1333-34].

3. Martham, Eaton, Sedgeford, Hemsby, Catton, Hindringham, 1471-72.

4. Martham, Eaton, Sedgeford, Catton, Hindringham, 1472-73.

5. Newton, Lathes, Sedgeford, Martham, Catton, Plumstead. With sheep accounts, 1475-76.

6. Hemsby, Hindolveston, Eaton, Lathes, Newton, Catton, Taverham, Sedgeford, Thornham, Plumstead, Pockthorpe, Martham, Elmham, 1477-78.

7. Hemsby, Martham, Plumstead, Catton, Pockthorpe, Newton, Eaton, Taverham, Hindolveston, Hindringham, Sedgeford, Thornham, Elmham, 1479-80.

8. Hindringham, Eaton, Taverham, Pockthorpe, Catton, Newton, Plumstead, Hindolveston, Sedgeford, Hemsby, Martham, Elmham, 1480-81.

9. Hindolveston, Thornham, Sedgeford, Elmham, Newton, Plumstead, Eaton, Catton, Martham, Hemsby, 1481-82.

10. Hindolveston, Sedgeford, Eaton, Lathes, Catton, Newton, 1482-83.

11. Lathes, Eaton, Newton, Hemsby, Plumstead, Elmham, Catton, Hindolveston, Hindringham, Sedgeford, 1484-85.

12. Lathes, Martham, Pockthorpe, Sedgeford, Gnatingdon, Plumstead, Eaton, Hindringham, Hemsby, Catton, 1485-86. With sheep accounts.

13. Heigham, Sedgeford, Eaton, Newton, Lathes, Berney, Hemsby, Martham, Hindolveston, Elmham, Gnatingdon, Hindringham, Taverham, 1486-87.

14. Sedgeford, Thornham, Plumstead, Catton, Eaton, Pockthorpe, Taverham, Newton, 1487-88.

15. Hindolveston, Elmham, Plumstead, Taverham, Newton, Hindringham, Catton, Martham, Hemsby, 1488-89. With sheep accounts.

16. This roll contains sheep accounts, 1488, 1493, 1494, 1499, 1500 and 1501 and bailiff's accounts for Pockthorpe, 1488; Plumstead, 1488; Thornham, 1494, 1499, 1500 and 1501 and Martham and Hemsby, 1500 and 1501.

17. Sedgeford, Pockthorpe, Martham, Hemsby, Hindringham, Newton, Heigham, 1490-91. With sheep accounts.

18. Eaton, Taverham, North Elmham, Martham, Hemsby, Sedgeford, Hindolveston, Catton, Plumstead, Newton, Pockthorpe, Hindringham, 1495-96.

19. North Elmham, Gateley, Hindringham, Plumstead, Catton, Sedgeford, Martham, Eaton, Lathes, 1496-97. With sheep accounts

20. Catton, Eaton, Plumstead, Hemsby, Martham, 1498-99.

21. Hindringham, Sedgeford, Thornham, Gateley, North Elmham, Catton, Pockthorpe, Newton, 1503-4.

22. Hemsby, Hindolveston, Martham, Newton, Pockthorpe, Sedgeford, North Elmham, Thorpe Episcopi, Hindringham, Lathes, Gnatingdon, Eaton, Plumstead, Catton, Thornham, Gateley, 1504-5. With sheep account.

22A. Prior's manors and Thorpe Episcopi, 1505-6.

23. Sedgeford, Gnatingdon, Thorpe, Newton, Hemsby, Martham, Hindolveston, Hindringham, Catton, Pockthorpe, Plumstead, Taverham, 1508-9. With sheep accounts.

24. Hemsby, Catton, Thornham, Sedgeford, Eaton, Plumstead, Pockthorpe, Taverham, Hindolveston, North Elmham, Gateley, Newton, Martham, Hindringham, 1509-10.

25. Pockthorpe, Hemsby, Sedgeford, Thornham, Martham, Catton, Hindringham, Hindolveston, North Elmham, 1510-11. With sheep accounts.

26. Arrears: Hindringham, Sedgeford, Catton, Eaton, Plumstead, 1511-12.

27. Sedgeford, Hindringham, Eaton, Thornham, Hindolveston, Martham, Newton, Pockthorpe, Gateley, North Elmham, Catton, Taverham, Plumstead, Hemsby, 1514-15.

28. Newton, North Elmham, Gateley, Plumstead, Hindolveston, Martham, Eaton, Catton, Taverham, Sedgeford, Thornham, 1515-16. With sheep accounts.

29. North Elmham, Gateley, Taverham, Catton, Newton, Martham, Eaton, Hemsby, Sedgeford, Hingringham, Hindolveston, Pockthorpe, 1516-17. With sheep account.

30. Hindringham, Eaton, Hemsby, Martham, North Elmham, Catton, Taverham, Plumstead, Hindolveston, Newton, 1527-28.

DCN 63/ GROUPED MANOR COURT BOOKS: NORWICH AND BROMHOLME

1. Grouped manor court book of Bromholme Priory covering manors in Bromholme, Bacton, Knapton, Witton, North Walsham, Worstead, Swaffield, Carleton Colville, [1525-40].

2. Grouped cathedral manor court book inscribed 'Miscellaneous Entries No 1'. Covers manors of Hindolveston, Hindringham, Sedgeford, Martham, Hemsby, Pockthorpe, Catton, Newton, Scratby, Thornham, North Elmham, Eaton, Normans, Wicklewood, Plumstead, Arminghall, Lakenham, Aldeby, [1503-8].

3. Grouped cathedral manor court book inscribed 'Miscellaneous Entries No 3.' Covers manors of Great Cressingham, Worstead, Hopton, Pockthorpe, Catton, Amners, [1618-25].

DCN 64/ MANOR ROLLS: SHEEP ACCOUNTS

1-12. Sheep accounts, 1485-1535.

DCN 65/ STEWARD'S MANORIAL ACCOUNTS, 1635-1849 (with gaps)

These list the fines paid to the Dean and Chapter at manorial courts. The manors covered are Great Cressingham, Aldeby, Eaton, Catton, Hindolveston, Hindringham, Trowse Newton, Pockthorpe, Normans, Anmers under the Oak, Worstead. The names of persons admitted are given. (137 docs)

DCN 66/ PROFITS OF MANORS AND ESTIMATIONS OF GRANGES

Prior's manors are Newton, Eaton, Taverham, Plumstead, Hemsby, Hindringham, Martham, Monks' Grange, Hindolveston, Gateley, Thornham, Sedgeford, Gnatington, Denham, Catton.

Obedientiaries' 'manors' in DCN 66/2 are churches or estates in Henley, Eaton, Bawburgh, Scratby, Lakenham, Arminghall, Stoke, Barford, Wiggenhall, Cressingham, Worstead, Martham, Hopton, Hemblington, Ormesby, Plumstead, Catton, Wicklewood, Attlebridge, Beckham, Creake, Witchingham, Monks' Grange, Chedgrave, Trowse, Strumpshaw. In DCN 66/5 they are the same manors except that Hemblington, Creake, Witchingham, Monks' Grange, and Chedgrave do not appear.

PROFITS OF MANORS

1. Prior's, 1281-87.
2. Prior's and obedientiaries', 1294-5.
3. Prior's, 1299-1302.
4. Prior's, 1302-3.
5. Obedientiaries', 1302-3.
6. Prior's, 1303-4.
7. Prior's, 1304-5.
8. Prior's, 1305-7.
9. Prior's, 1307-8.
10. Prior's, ?1331-2.
11. Part only, obedientiaries', n.d.

ESTIMATIONS OF THE GRANGES

12. 1298-9.
13. 1299-1300.
14. 1304-5.
15. 1306-7.
16. 1332-3.
17. 1333-4.
18. 1334-5, 1336-41.
19. 1341-2.
20. 1346-7.

PECULIAR ADMINISTRATION

Dean and Chapter Peculiar administration extended over the parishes of Arminghall, West Beckham, Catton, Hindolveston, Martham, Norwich St Mary in the Marsh (which included the Cathedral Precinct), Norwich St Helen, Norwich St James Pockthorpe, Norwich St Paul, Eaton, Lakenham, Great Plumstead, Sedgeford, Sprowston and Trowse and before the Reformation only of Hindringham, Scratby, Taverham and Winterton.

The Peculiar was exempt from the Archdeacons' jurisdiction, but not from that of the Bishop.

Many records of the Dean and Chapter Peculiar administration passed to diocesan officials as a result of administrative changes after 1812, and are now listed with the main series of diocesan records held by the Norfolk Record Office.

Visitations within the Dean and Chapter Peculiar are recorded in the Norwich Archdeaconry series for the period 1545-83.

DCN 67/ RECORDS OF PECULIAR ADMINISTRATION

ACTA AND COMPERTA ROLLS: records of visitation by Priory officials of the parishes within its jurisdiction. About 150 wills are endorsed on the back of these rolls: these are indexed in *Norfolk Genealogy,* xvi.

1.	1416, 1417.
2.	1417.
3.	1419, 1420.
4.	1421-3.
5.	1427.
6.	1428, 1429.
7.	1429 (inventory of utensils at Hindolveston Manor, with wills).
8.	1430, 1433.
9.	1434-7.
9A.	1435 (Hindolveston only).
10.	1436.
11.	1452.

DCN 68/ MARRIAGE LICENCE BONDS

1.	1705-24.
2.	1848-60.
3.	Marriage licence bond of James Sanders of Upwell, 1799.

DCN 69/ REGISTERS OF WILLS AND ADMINISTRATIONS

1. 1444-54.
2. 1461-1559.

DCN 70/ ORIGINAL WILLS

1. 1577, 1585-1609.
2. Bundle of miscellaneous wills, many not proved in Dean and Chapter court, with related documents, 1291-1944.

DCN 71/ ADMINISTRATION ACT BOOK

1. 1613-80. (For act books 1444-1559 see DCN 69.)

DCN 72/ ADMINISTRATION BONDS

1. 1706-37.

DCN 73/ PROBATE INVENTORIES

1. 1681-6.
2. 1687-94.
3. 1717 (one only).
4. 1723-37.
5. 1737-82.

DCN 74/ CORONER'S INQUESTS

1-17. Bundle of coroner's inquests, 1568-1738.

(Coroner's inquests, 1799-1899, are filed with Precinct Sessions papers: see DCN 82/9.)

DCN 75/ PENANCES AND RETRACTIONS

1. Penances and retractions for adultery, fornication before marriage, incest, defamation, 1682-1738. (*c.*50 docs)

DCN 76/ VISITATION RECORDS

1, 2. General visitation books, 1774-1811.
3-22. Visitation of parishes in the peculiar, 1772-1811.
23-29. Visitation papers, 1520-1847.
30, 31. Seal fees, 1782-1832.

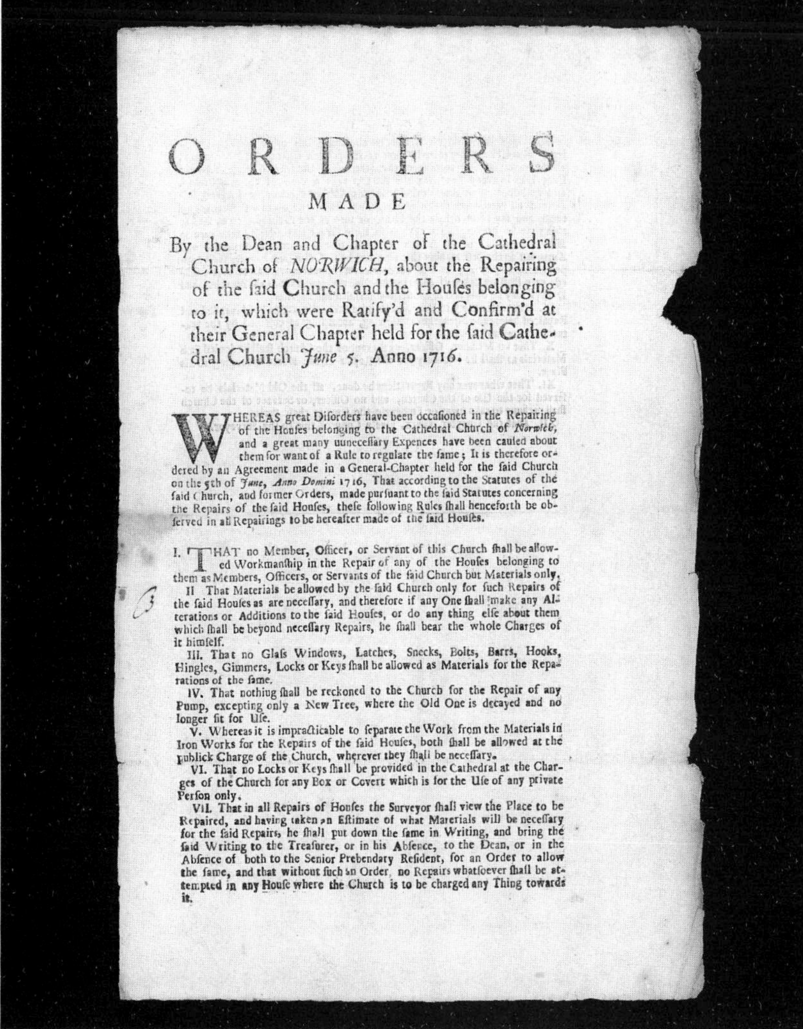

ORDERS
MADE

By the Dean and Chapter of the Cathedral Church of *NORWICH*, about the Repairing of the ſaid Church and the Houſes belonging to it, which were Ratify'd and Confirm'd at their General Chapter held for the ſaid Cathedral Church *June* 5. Anno 1716.

WHEREAS great Diſorders have been occaſioned in the Repairing of the Honſes belonging to the Cathedral Church of *Norwich*, and a great many uunecceſſary Expences have been cauſed about them for want of a Rule to regulate the ſame; It is therefore ordered by an Agreement made in a General-Chapter held for the ſaid Church on the 5th of *June*, *Anno Domini* 1716, That according to the Statutes of the ſaid Church, and former Orders, made purſuant to the ſaid Statutes concerning the Repairs of the ſaid Houſes, theſe following Rules ſhall henceforth be obſerved in all Repairings to be hereafter made of the ſaid Houſes.

I. THAT no Member, Officer, or Servant of this Church ſhall be allowed Workmanſhip in the Repair of any of the Houſes belonging to them as Members, Officers, or Servants of the ſaid Church but Materials only.

II That Materials be allowed by the ſaid Church only for ſuch Repairs of the ſaid Houſes as are neceſſary, and therefore if any One ſhall make any Alterations or Additions to the ſaid Houſes, or do any thing elſe about them which ſhall be beyond neceſſary Repairs, he ſhall bear the whole Charges of it himſelf.

III. That no Glaſs Windows, Latches, Snecks, Bolts, Barrs, Hooks, Hingles, Gimmers, Locks or Keys ſhall be allowed as Materials for the Reparations of the ſame.

IV. That nothiug ſhall be reckoned to the Church for the Repair of any Pump, excepting only a New Tree, where the Old One is decayed and no longer fit for Uſe.

V. Whereas it is impracticable to ſeparate the Work from the Materials in Iron Works for the Repairs of the ſaid Houſes, both ſhall be allowed at the publick Charge of the Church, wherever they ſhall be neceſſary.

VI. That no Locks or Keys ſhall be provided in the Cathedral at the Charges of the Church for any Box or Covert which is for the Uſe of any private Perſon only.

VII. That in all Repairs of Houſes the Surveyor ſhall view the Place to be Repaired, and having taken an Eſtimate of what Materials will be neceſſary for the ſaid Repairs, he ſhall put down the ſame in Writing, and bring the ſaid Writing to the Treaſurer, or in his Abſence, to the Dean, or in the Abſence of both to the Senior Prebendary Reſident, for an Order to allow the ſame, and that without ſuch an Order, no Repairs whatſoever ſhall be attempted in any Houſe where the Church is to be charged any Thing towards it.

After the priory was dissolved in 1538, the Close became just like any other part of the city, with workshops and public houses. From the early eighteenth century the chapter began to assert more control and bring about a slow 'gentrification' of the area. *DCN 107/7*

DCN 77/ ADMINISTRATION RECORDS

1. Commissary court book, 1769-1855.
2. Case papers, 1800-55.
3. Minute book, 1841-55.
4. Faculty book, 1761-1842.

5-22. Papers and notes re peculiar jurisdiction, 18th and 19th centuries.

DCN 77A Consolidations of Norwich parishes, 1564-1877. (7 docs)

DCN 78 Bonds of Obligation to prior and convent, 1343-1536 (10 docs) and to Dean and Chapter, 1549-1777 (31 docs).

PRECINCT JURISDICTION

DCN 79/ **HOLMSTREET LEET COURT AND FAIR COURT ROLLS, 1429-1500**

HOLMSTREET LEET

1. Tuesday after Trinity, 1429.
2. Tuesday after Trinity, 1437.
3. Tuesday after Trinity, 1440, 1441.
4. Tuesday after Trinity, 1442, 1443.
5. Tuesday after Trinity, 1444, 1445.

FAIR COURTS

6. Fair court: Pentecost and Trinity, 1422.
7. Fair court: Pentecost and Trinity, 1432.
8. Fair court: Pentecost and Trinity, 1436.
9. Fair court: Pentecost and Trinity, 1442.
10. Fair court: Pentecost and Trinity, 1452.
11. Pie Powder Court, Pentecost, 1498. On dorse, Holmestreet leet court, Tuesday after Trinity, 1498.
12. Pie Powder Court, Pentecost, 1500.

DCN 80 **SHERIFF'S WARRANTS** (for collections of amercements, etc.), 1476-1547.

DCN 81 **SESSIONS ROLLS,** 1580, 1611-20 (with gaps), 1718-1831.

DCN 82 **SESSIONS PAPERS,** 1746-1889. With oath of allegiance to King George 1723 and miscellaneous papers. Sessions papers, 1799-1889, include inquests.

DCN 83 **ALEHOUSE LICENCES** (alehouses in the precinct), 1801-28, 1838. With recognizances of beer-drawers, 1733, 1735.

LEGAL DOCUMENTS

DCN 84 Ecclesiastical courts, county and out-county, *c.*1206-1444. (43 docs)

DCN 85 Ecclesiastical courts, Norwich, 1276-1523. (20 docs)

DCN 86 Civil and criminal courts, 1289-1535. (31 docs)

DCN 87 Disputes, agreements with Carmelites in Norwich and Lynn, 1376-1460. (6 docs)

DCN 88 Disputes, agreements with Carrow Abbey, 1319-1419. (15 docs)

DCN 88A Agreement with St Mary in the Fields, Norwich, 1281. (1 doc)

DCN 89 Disputes, agreements between Cathedral and the City 1205-1524, 1601-1715 (24 docs)

DCN 90 Lawsuits re disputed leases, et*c.*, 17th and 18th centuries. (19 bundles)

DCN 91 Miscellaneous legal papers, 17th-19th centuries. (19 docs)

EPISCOPAL AND DIOCESAN

DCN 92/ BISHOP'S VISITATIONS OF THE CATHEDRAL

1. Injunctions at visitation, 1308.
2. Injunctions at visitation, 1319.

3-29. Injunctions, supporting papers re visitations, 1570-1905.

DCN 93/ DIOCESAN PATENT BOOKS

Appointments and leases confirmed by the dean and chapter.

1. 1541-66.
2. 1566-1621.

[3. 1621-67, in private hands. A microfilm copy is available in the Norfolk Record Office].

4. 1667-1768.
5. 1770-1904.

DCN 94/ SEQUESTRATION BOOK AND CAVEAT BOOK

1. Register of grants of sequestration, 1808-80. In back, Caveat Book (record of decrees that no will be proved or administration granted until an interested party has been heard), 1788-1868.

DCN 95/ DIOCESAN, INCLUDING ST BENET'S ABBEY

A varied collection of documents, some clearly strays from the diocesan archives, the status of others uncertain. With two documents from St Benet's, also presumably from the diocesan records.

OLD FOUNDATION

1. Ordinations: records of some 40 ordinations, 1362-1406.
2. Torn and incomplete document issued by Richard, prior of Holy Trinity, Norwich, relating to episcopal obedience, 1264.
3. Bishop J. of Norwich presents Michael Peikirk to church of Stanford at presentation of Shouldham priory, 23 August 1301.
4. Bailiff's account, Battisford (Suffolk), 1326-7.
5. Bailiff's account, Hoxne (Suffolk), 1326-7.
6. Bailiff's account, Thornage, 1326-7.
7. Bailiff's account, North Elmham, 1326-7.
8. Castleward account of John de Wychingham: list of knights' fees of the bishop on which castleward paid, 1327-8.

9. Bailiff's account, North Elmham, 1328-9.
10. Bailiff's account, Gaywood, 1330.
11. Bailiff's account, Hevingham, 1330-1.
12. Receipts from bishop's manors, 1330-1.
13. Bailiff's account, Lynn, 1331-2.
14. Bailiff's account, Strumpshaw, n.d.
15. Eaton next Honingham: agreement to pay 12d a year from church of college of St Mary in the Fields in Norwich to Archdeacon of Norfolk, 1365.
16. Institution to Dickleburgh church on resignation of Simon Smythe, on nomination of monastery of Bury St Edmunds, 1402.
17. Notification by bishop of Norwich of institution of John Grynnel of Hereford diocese to Little Carbrooke, 1403.
18. Induction of John Burton to deanery of Lynn on resignation of John Stanford, 1406.
19. Account of bailiff of knight's fees of the bishop, 1420-1.
20. Account of reeve and messor of Hoxne (Suffolk), 1445-6.
21. Account roll of the bishop's receiver, 1462-3.
22. Account of bailiff of knight's fees of the bishop, 1470-1.
23. Bailiff's account for Hoe and Beetley, Michaelmas, 1537-8.

NEW FOUNDATION

24. Manor court roll, Horning, 1628.
25. Page of subscriptions to liturgy of Church of England, 1718.
26. Bundle of diocesan papers, including application and licence to teach for Edward Scott, 1721; declaration of James Stagg on institution to Welborne, 1722; also of John Hardy on institution to Bintry, 1721; note of appointment of Samuel Gall to curacy of Langham, 1719.
27. Bundle of letters re episcopal jurisdiction over Emneth 18th century; with list of presentations to parishes in Norwich diocese, 1738-47.
28. Visitation fee book, 14 June-19 July [1716].
29. Account book, fees of secretary of Bishop of Norwich (William Utten, secretary to Bishop Sutton), 1790-1809; with attorney's fees in cases of disputed faculties, testamentary cases, etc., 1769-1810.
30. Account book of Bishop Sutton, 1800-10 (1 volume).
31. Faculty of Archbishop of Canterbury to pull down stable and outbuildings adjoining Bishop's Palace, 1838.

ST BENET'S

32. Rental of estate of St Benet's Abbey in Worstead, [late 14th century?].

33. Bailiff's account, Hellesdon, 1459-60.

CHARITIES, SCHOLARS AND SCHOOLS

DCN 96 Payments to Poor account book, 1759-1910, with miscellaneous charity papers.

DCN 97 Norris Charity for felons in the Castle - account book, 1782-1890, with related papers.

DCN 98 Norman and Simon charities - appointment of Dean Turner as trustee for Norman charity, 1790; receipts from disbursements under Mr Simons's charity for clergymen's widows, 1742-67.

DCN 99 Norwich Charity Schools - deeds, papers, et*c*., mainly re Boys' Model School in St Peter Hungate, Norwich, 19th and 20th centuries.

DCN 100 Returns of maintained scholars at Trinity College, Cambridge, 1582-1683 and at Gonville and Caius College, Cambridge, 1581-1680.

DCN 101 Cathedral Choir School - papers and notes of Canon E. A. Parr, 19th and 20th centuries.

THE CATHEDRAL FABRIC

DCN 102 Salvin papers, 1830-6.

DCN 103 Restoration of west front, 1870s.

DCN 104 Repairs to tower and spire, 1883-6.

DCN 105 Other 19th-century works: Bishop Pelham memorial throne, 1894-5; organ and organ case, 1888-9; restoration of cloisters, 1873.

DCN 106 War memorial chapel, 1915-32.

DCN 107 Miscellaneous papers re repairs, restoration work, 1607-1942, including organ accounts, 1607-9, Cathedral Repairs account, 1660.

DCN 108 Reparation, organ and visitors' fund papers, 1885-1929.

THE CATHEDRAL SERVICES

DCN 109 Services: registers and service forms with report on music in the Cathedral, 1841-1991.

DCN 110 Registers of attendance of Canons, 1851-69, 1910-43.

DCN 111 Cathedral inventories, 1704-1949.

DCN 112 Cathedral monumental inscriptions.

DEANS' PERSONAL PAPERS

DCN 113 DEAN SUCKLING (1614-28): 'Dean Suckling's Book' - copies of charters, statutes, et*c*.

DCN 114 DEAN CROFTS (1660-70): letters to Crofts. (3 docs)

DCN 115/ DEAN PRIDEAUX (1702-24):

1-3. Diaries (detailed record of chapter business), 1694-1724. (3 vols)
4-11. Collections and transcriptions of historical material relating to the Cathedral and also to Norwich city, Yarmouth and Bury St Edmunds. (8 docs)
12. Letters to Prideaux, 1701-23. (6 docs)

DCN 116 DEAN COLE (1724-31): letters to Cole. (2 docs)

DCN 117 DEAN BULLOCK (1739-60): letters to Bullock and one from him. (18 docs)

DCN 118/ DEAN LLOYD (1765-90):

1. Memoranda (notes re cathedral events), 1767-80.
2. *Notitia* (account of benefices of Dean and Chapter taken from Tanner's indexes to the bishop's registers).
3. Repertory of cathedral archives, 1780.
4. Letter book (copies of incoming letters), 1770-89.
5. Out-letter book, 1767-90.
6. Diary of visit to Italy, written by unnamed companion of Dean Lloyd, 1788.
7. Copy of *Valor Ecclesiasticus* late 16th century/early 17th century, with later index.
8. Letters to Lloyd (8 docs).

DCN 119 DEAN TURNER (1790-1828): letters to Turner (11 docs).

DCN 120 DEAN PELLEW (1828-66):

1/1-7. Diaries and notes re chapter proceedings.
1/8. Library catalogue, 1836.
2. Letters to Pellew, many with draft of his reply (*c.*1,500 letters).
3. Letters to Pellew re William Smyth memorial window (113 letters).

DCN 121/ DEAN GOULBURN (1866-89):

1. Out-letter book, 1868-74.
2. Detailed notes of chapter proceedings, 1886-9.
3. Printed works by Goulburn.
4. Letters to Goulburn (*c*.30 docs).

DCN 122 DEAN LEFROY (1889-1909): letters to Lefroy (*c*.40 docs).

DCN 123 DEAN BEECHING (1911-19): sermons and antiquarian notes (35 vols).

DCN 124 DEAN WILLINK (1919-27): letter to Willink (1 doc).

MISCELLANEOUS

DNC 125/ ANTIQUARIAN PAPERS

1. 'Antiquarian Records of Norwich Cathedral, vol. 1: The Cathedral': scrapbook of sketches of cathedral by Mrs Evans and Mrs Symonds and many others of which the artist is not known, 19th century.

2. 'Antiquarian Records of Norwich Cathedral, vol. 2: The Deanery': scrapbook of sketches of Deanery and also of Cathedral and of Erpingham Gate, 19th century.

3. Photograph album of Norwich Cathedral retable with historical notes. Presented to the cathedral by E. C. Le Grice, 1968.

4-33. Antiquarian notes and related papers including transcript by John Kirkpatrick of cellarer's roll of 1318-19 [DCN 125/6], manuscript 'Memoir of Dean Pellew and Dr Zechariah Buck' by Edward Symonds, late 19th century.

DCN 126/ NON-CATHEDRAL RECORDS

1. Deeds and papers of Thurlow family [Edward Thurlow was prebend, 1788-1847], 1786-1847.

2. Legal papers and deeds from the office of Matthew and William Rackham and John Kitson [John Kitson was chapter clerk, 1812-69; Matthew Rackham was auditor 1822-60], 1788-1851.

3. Papers of Bensly and Bolingbroke, solicitors [Dr Bensly succeeded Kitson as chapter clerk in 1870]. Papers relate mainly to the Hotblack family of Norwich and Brighton.

4. Miscellaneous non-cathedral papers, including a list of liberties of Norwich merchants [in French, 14th century].

DCN 127/ MAPS AND PLANS

1. Survey of precincts and Bishop's Palace, showing line of proposed railway, 1881.

2. 20th-century reconstruction of plan of cathedral, monastic buildings and Bishop's Palace.

3. 'Section of presbytery in two states' (i.e., with and without flying buttresses), n.d.

4. Drawing of Bishop's Throne, Torcello, n.d.

5. Drawing of Bishop's throne in the same hand as DCN 127/4, n.d.

6. Plan of parish of Arminghall. Fields named, numbered, acreages given, church and house by common in elevation, 1779.

7. 20th-century plan of the cathedral, to show dates of fabric.

8. Plan of parish of Hemblington, fields numbered, no reference book, 1838.

9. Plan of chapter estate in Acle and Foldholme and Skeetholme Marshes, fields numbered, acreages given, 1890.

10. Plan of chapter estate in Eaton, attached to lease of North Farm, Eaton, by Dean and Chapter to Jonathan Davey, 1806.

11. Plan of Gascoines and Lines estate in Norwich Cathedral precinct, [18th century].

12. Plan of proposed triptych reredos incorporating medieval panels for St Saviour's Chapel, Norwich Cathedral. Plan by J. Dykes Bower, [20th century].

13. Ground plan of North Elmham cathedral, [20th century].

14-16. Detailed plans of cathedral spire and tower. W. Haslop, 1952-4.

17. Plan of chapter estate in Field Dalling and Bale, 1813.

18. Plan of chapter estate in Thorpe next Norwich, 1803.

19. Plan of chapter estate in Foldholme and Skeetholme marshes near Yarmouth, 1733.

20. Plan of estate of Revd John Humfrey in the Close and Tombland, 1834.

21. Plan of Arminghall Hall Farm in Arminghall and Caister parishes, [1743-72].

22, 23. Two copies of plan of Arminghall parish, 1813.

24. Plan of chapter estate in St James Pockthorpe and St Paul, Norwich, [19th century].

25. Copy of south-west view of Cathedral as drawn by J. Buckler, [19th century].

26. Plans for reconstruction of north transept roof of the Cathedral. B. M. Fielden, 1956.

27. Plan of chapter estate in Attlebridge and Swannington, 1730.

28, 29. Two sets of designs for proposed new chapel at east end of Cathedral. Charles Nicholson, 1917 and 1927.

30. Plans for new house in the Close. Charles J. Brown, 1896.

31. Plan of house and garden in Blofield belonging to Robert Crane, 1828.

32. Drawings of 'section of edge of pit' and 'mosaic floor', location not identified, 1906.

33A. Plan to show south-east boundary of Yarmouth churchyard, [19th century].

33B. Plan for Gothic design to house the cathedral clock, [19th century].

34. Plan of St Faiths Lane, Norwich to show proposed new passage into the Close [19th century].

35. Plan of Hellesdon parsonage. W. T. Spurgeon, 1952.

36. Copy of south part of Eaton tithe map, [19th century].

37. Copies of plan of chapter offices in the Close. Francis Stone, 1818.

38. Copy of Martham tithe map, [19th century].

39. Plans of chapter estate in St Pauls, Norwich showing building lots, 1824-54.

40. Plan of cottages in Broadwater Lane in the Close, occupiers' names given, [19th century].

41. Plan of warehouse beside river in Norwich to show line of proposed new building, [post 1828].

42. Plans of houses adjoining 'Clarke's house and garden' in unnamed street, [post 1805].

43. Tracings probably from tithe map of Thorpe next Norwich, [19th century].

44. Plan of Mr Dersley's garden in St Peter Parmountergate, Norwich, 1781.

45. Tracing of plan of lands in Thorpe between Bishop Bridge and Foundry Bridge, [mid-19th century].

46. Two plans of Gogill's Gardens adjoining St Peter Parmountergate churchyard, Norwich, [19th century].

47. Plan of Dean and Chapter estate outside Magdalen Gates, Norwich, [late 19th century].

48. Plan of fields in Horning, showing land usage, [18th century].

49. Plans, elevations, section of Hopton parsonage, Suffolk. Abel Tillett of Yarmouth. With supporting papers, [*c.*1842].

50. Plans and specifications, alterations to Canon Nevill's house in the Close, Norwich, 1873.

51. Plan and section, east end of unidentified church, [19th century].

52. Mr Deteor's plan of unidentified house and yard, no notation, [19th century].

53. Plans, elevations and sections, The Dial House, The Close, Norwich by Charles J. Brown, 1904.

54, 55. Plans of Aldeby rectory, showing parts to be taken down, proposed new buildings, [*c.*1830], with related papers.

56. Coloured tracing of land along edge of Lower Close adjoining the Horsefair, showing proposed new road, [19th century].

57. Floor plan, no 3, The Close, Norwich, [19th century].

58. Plan of no 7, The Close, Norwich, 1937.

59. Plan and two letters re 70 Bishopgate, Norwich, 1946-9.

60. Plan and elevations, The Vicarage House, Worstead, by J. C. and G. Buckler, 1841.

61. Specifications for work done for Revd J. Thurlow at Hindringham Vicarage House, with plans and elevations, [1843-44].

62. Alterations and additions to Canon Nisbet's House by John H. Brown, 1873 and by James K. Colling, 1880.

63. Plan of Oxford or Town Meadow, Worstead. Surveyor: Robert Wymer, 1784.

64-66. Plans of proposed restorations of cloisters by J. H. Brown, [*c.*1873].

67. Elevation, Henley Vicarage House, Suffolk and plan of pightle and garden, [19th century].

68. Sketch for alterations in layout of Upper Close proposed by Mr Kitson, [19th century].

69. Elevation and plan of gallery of unidentified church, endorsed 'Mr Worthy, Trowse', [*c.*1846].

70-72. Plans of estates of Dean and Chapter and of J. E. Lacon in Ormesby, [early 19th century].

73. Elevation and section of walling of unidentified tower, [late 19th century].

74-77. Plans and book of reference, Dean and Chapter estate at Hindringham, 1739.

78. Plan of glebe land and land of Revd J. R. E. Nelson in Congham, 1839.

79. Copy of Halvergate tithe map, no apportionment, [19th century].

80. Plan of St Leonard's Pieces in parish of St Clement, Norwich, the property of the Dean and Chapter. Surveyor: Robert Wymer, 1781.

81. Plan of proposed factory in St Mary's Norwich, for H. J. Sexton, drawn by Edward Boardman and Son, [*c.*1919].

Work on the south-east part of the Cathedral during one of the late nineteenth-century restorations. The statues of the apostles on the tops of the flying buttresses are nineteenth-century copies of the fifteenth-century originals.
DCN 131/46

DCN 128/ WATERCOLOURS

1-4. Watercolours of interior and exterior of the Cathedral by David Hodgson, 1830-2.

DCN 129/ SEALS, SEAL MATRICES, ARTEFACTS

1-11. 13th-century seal matrix of the Cathedral (front only), with later seals and matrices and artefacts including 5 'prickle-pens' and labels on wood from chests in which archives were once stored.

DCN 130/ XEROXES OF DCN RECORDS

1-12. Xerox copies of cathedral records including some of originals which are too fragile to use.

DCN 131/ PAPERS OF CATHEDRAL SURVEYORS

1-234. Records found in the office of Arthur Bensly Whittingham, surveyor to the fabric, 1933-63, including records of his predecessors John Brown (1830s-1869), John Henry Brown (1869-91), John Charles Brown (1891-1932). The documents include some drawings from the architectural practices of John Brown and John Henry Brown.

1996 DEPOSIT

DCN 132 LETTER BOOKS, 1888-1940.

DCN 133 FINANCIAL - CASH BOOKS AND LEDGERS, 1840-1950.

DCN 134 FINANCIAL - COLLECTIONS ACCOUNTS, 1900-60.

DCN 135 FINANCIAL - BANK BOOKS, 1882-1932.

DCN 136 FINANCIAL - INVOICES, 1986-7.

DCN 137 ESTATE PAPERS - THE CLOSE, 1803-1954.

DCN 138 ESTATE PAPERS - CITY ESTATES, 1824-48.

DCN 139 ESTATE PAPERS - COUNTRY ESTATES, 1870-1938.

DCN 140 CATHEDRAL VISITORS' BOOKS, 1885-1907.

DCN 141 SERVICE REGISTERS, 1920-84.

DCN 142 SPECIAL SERVICE FORMS, 1882, 1962-93.

DCN 143 SACRIST'S CORRESPONDENCE FILES, 1978-93.

DCN 144 SACRIST'S OFFICE DIARIES, 1953-93.

DCN 145 ANTIQUARIAN RECORDS.

DCN 146 LEGAL MEMORANDA, 1895-1934.

DCN 147 THE BOOK OF REMEMBRANCE [Listing soldiers killed in the First World War].

DCN 148 CATHEDRAL REFERENCE BOOK.

DCN 149 WILLS OF THE DEAN AND MRS GOULBURN, *c*.1868-*c*.1889.

DCN 150 DIOCESAN AND EPISCOPAL, 1823-1941.

DCN 151 CONGÉ D' ÉLIRE, 1985.

DCN 152 SOLICITORS' PAPERS, 1802-1909.

DCN 153 PLANS, 1961.